To my father . . .
who taught me to be quiet

CONTENTS

STENELLA

Wild Dolphin project

There is nothing like the first encounter with a dolphin in the wild. It is an unexpected delight to be with something this special. Before breakfast I walked onto the deck and spotted a "fin" moving through the waves a few yards from the stern of the boat. "Dolphins!" I called. We plunged over the side of *Stenella*, a 62' catamaran, into the midst of a pod of spotted dolphins. Within seconds I found myself just "hanging" next to a male (later identified as Skew) watching, observing and being observed. The fact that they will come so close . . . amazing. How comfortable I have become with jumping off the side of a boat into the water because the call of dolphins goes out. How quickly I ignore the fact we saw a large tiger shark in these same waters just yesterday.

My mind wants to label the dolphins good and the shark bad when, in fact, they are both parts of nature . . . the yin and the yang of it. The shark has as much right to be here as the dolphins, he (or she) also has a story to tell.

Intuitions was originally published in 1988, telling of my initial encounters with expanded awareness—from my childhood into the early '80's. With this present edition my life has moved in many new (and yet similar) directions.

As life continues to unfold I constantly remind myself that what has become "normal" to me actually, isn't normal to many individuals, but falls into the category of "make believe." Here, in the early 1990's many things are taking place very rapidly on the planet, a new awareness of GAIA, of looking for something more . . . a connection to the earth. The cold war is over and people are talking about their search for meaning.

Things are changing. The question is are we ready for the change and can we meet the challenge? Can we change our way of thinking, suspend our disbeliefs and create new paradigms in order to meet the challenge?

The Second Edition of *Intuitions* wouldn't be complete without a section on the environment, and for me, perhaps my biggest mentors . . . dolphins. I once heard Kelli McGee, one of the educators at the Dolphin Research Center say, "The dolphins call us, and when they do you can't hang up."

In 1990 Michael (my partner) became interested in dolphins. He has always been an advocate of wildlife and fascinated with nature—especially with the ocean and its mysteries. Through a series of synchronistic events he found himself in a program at the *Dolphin Research Center* in the Florida Keys. He immediately saw the connection between the world of the dolphins and the world of the sixth sense, so as a result, we began to combine our workshop on intuition with a week-long dolphin swim.

"What is it like to be with the dolphins?" you might ask.

To which I would reply, "I really can't tell you, you'll just have to experience them for yourselves."

When I first met the dolphins I had given very little thought as to why so many individuals wanted to swim with them. I probably felt that they were similar to most animals with whom we have a great telepathic rapport. However, to recount all of the ways that dolphins have shown me there is more to our Universe than meets the eye would take a book in itself, and couldn't do justice to them or to my experience. I can say that there has been more than one occasion when the dolphin I was with very clearly read my mind.

My first experience of "dolphin telepathy" was with Annessa, a dolphin that, I soon learned, loved to tease and "stretch" humans in many different ways.

Annessa and her lagoon partner Aleta had just given me a long dorsal pull, practically taking me to Cuba from Grassy Key. After (finally) deciding that it was time to obey their trainer's whistle, they tipped their rostrum down, their massive gray bodies descended below the surface, and my hand slipped from their dorsal fins.

"I'm so far out here, why don't they take me back?" No sooner than this thought formed than I felt Annessa push her fin against the palm of my hand. Words could not have made the message any clearer: "Take hold and I'll take you back!" I knew then, from the depth of my being, that there was much more to dolphins than I had imagined . . . ever.

Two other experiences that week showed me just how elementary we humans are at communication. My next "wake-up came with Natua, the most practiced at being in movies, and the center of much of the research into dolphins' understanding human language.

This time I was trying my hand (and signals) at being a dolphin trainer. When Natua didn't respond, I was perplexed because I knew he understood what I was asking him to do.

Suddenly, a total knowing swept over me and a picture within a picture within a picture came into my awareness. Natua told me I was asking him to perform a behavior that didn't make sense. (I had verbally asked Natua to execute a flip, yet I was signaling for him to dive.) He also, very gently, pointed out where we were in the grand scheme of things . . ." little me" and the rest of the cosmos.

Swedenborg, a seventeenth century Swedish mathematician, who communicated with the "angels" when he meditated, described their communication as a telepathic burst of knowledge, a picture language so dense that each image contained a thousand ideas. This was the way Natua had communicated with me in that moment.

Now I knew that not only could dolphins read my mind, but also I could understand their telepathic messages (each image containing a thousand ideas.) How little we know about the workings of our own mind and how little we know about the mind of the dolphin.

The final experience of my first week with dolphins came with Misty. Misty is an older dolphin and one that can frequently be contrary. All week Misty had preferred the absence of humans and had demonstrated this by hanging out in the far corner of her pool. On this particular morning she called to me, using her signature whistle, as I was walking down the lane. I was so surprised I didn't believe that it was Misty, but Deb (one of the DRC staff) yelled to me, "Misty is calling you."

I tentatively moved over to Misty's dock and sat down. I waited.

Nothing. I waited longer. Nothing.

Finally, after twenty minutes or more, I decided to try to communicate with her by placing a single, clear thought (this simplicity was for me, not her) in the center of my mind and sending it out. It was awkward, trying to formulate a question that would be appropriate, respectful, and not too much trouble for her. (Trouble for her? What a joke!) At the same time, I was anxious to know if she could or would *read* my mind and respond.

"Misty, I really hate to ask you to do this, but I am trying to understand how to communicate with you, and, ummm, would you mind, horribly . . . I mean I know you probably don't feel like it, but would you mind? If you can understand me, would you please swim by the dock to show me that this stuff works?" *She would, and she did.*

More recently I have been spending all of my free time with Marina who is attempting to teach me dolphin communication.

Annessa, Natua, Misty, and Marina all led up to this week, far beyond the sight of land, somewhere on the waters off the Bahamas. Watching the contour of the emerald green water, I realized that I sense when dolphins are near, even if I can't consciously hear or see them.

"Now," you might ask, "Why is there a chapter on dolphins in a book on intuition? Why talk about dolphins in the forward to the book?"

Because dolphins show us our connectedness, something we need to get back in touch with if we are to survive, just like our intuition. It's all the same. We are them and they are us. In 1973 Carl Sagan wrote:

"If we can't understand dolphins in their environment, with their intelligence, how can we expect to understand a being who comes from another planet, someone we wish to call alien?"

I am now, more than ever, convinced that the word *intuition* has a depth to it, just as the dolphins have a depth to them, that we will probably never understand, no matter how much we study and observe them, or how much we study and observe our intuition.

Approach your intuition gently, just as you would approach a dolphin. Come into her environment with an openness to discover what's there. Listen. Learn *her* language.

Our intuition points to our deep desire to connect, just as the dolphins want to connect. Use your curiosity, your desire to know, to understand, to discover your inner world.

And, if the dolphins call you, know that you won't be able to hang up, not now . . . not ever.

PART ONE

Introduction

"Toto I've a feeling we're not in Kansas anymore."
—Dorothy in *The Wizard of Oz*

IF YOU BELIEVE IN FAIRY TALES . . .

Once upon a time when dreams came true and imaginary playmates were something to be "reckoned" with, there lived a little girl who lived in a house in the woods with her parents. Quite often the little girl would wander the woods with her friends (that only she could see) playing Indian or, better yet, "Little Red RidingHood." In those days' magic was an everyday occurrence, for the little girl could summon up rainstorms at will, or make well almost any of God's creatures that found the good fortune to be at her healing hands. (After marrying a wildlife rehabilitator, I learned that I was probably using an intuitive knowing of what was needed, righting an unconscious bird and holding it in the warmth of my hands, for instance.)

On days when she was very, very lucky, her father would take her fishing. It was there that he taught her to be quiet. Otherwise she would not be able to hear the fish when they wished to talk with her.

On the days when she was not so lucky her father would head off to the golf course to have a "round" of golf. "My dear," he would say, "Golf is like the game of life. Every round is a journey which ultimately leads you back to exactly where you began. The ball is a symbol of perfection in that it contains all potential because it is a sphere. When it is in flight it is a reminder to us that we can fly, if we but put our minds to it. If you can learn to focus your mind, and send that little white ball exactly where you want it to go, then you can focus your life and create it exactly as you would have it be. Do not begrudge me my game of golf, for there in that simple game is the possibility of finding the true secret of life."

I was that little girl.

There would be times when my parents and I would pack our bags and head off to Georgia to visit my grandparents. This trip was likely to take place any time during the year, always on a moment's notice, when my father decided he could leave his business for a few days. It never failed that when we would arrive dinner would be waiting, hot, on the table. This in itself always amazed me because we had been driving for hours and I knew that we hadn't called to tell my grandmother when we would arrive. In fact, she didn't have a telephone. When I would ask how did she know to have dinner on the table, my parents would reply, "She just knows." Yet, she didn't even *know*, rationally, on what day we would arrive.

It would not be unusual during our visit for my grandmother to refer to the noise upstairs as being made by someone who had long since "left this plane" or to speak of seeing the "fairies dancing in the rain." All of this was very normal to me, and my parents were wise enough not to say whether they did, or didn't, believe in what grandmother said.

I quickly discovered, once I started school, that other children didn't believe in ghosts and fairies. I was definitely in the minority.

Those first years of school were difficult for me.

Whenever the teacher would write a math problem on the board, I always knew the answer, but I didn't have a clue as to how to "solve" the problem, so I was always accused of cheating. I would also be accused of eavesdropping because I would know things that I shouldn't know. "If you hadn't been listening you wouldn't know this." I soon learned it was best to keep my mouth shut and not say what I knew or thought.

As I look back through my childhood, I can remember just "knowing things" but not relating this knowledge to psychic ability. I remember the time I knew that a lost child was sitting on the side of a lily pool and if I didn't get to him, he would fall in and drown. I thought I was able to stand in my yard and look down at the pond and see him, but in reality there was no way I could stand in my yard, look through the forest and down a hill and see him.

I remember, "knowing" a childhood friend was going to die, and when he did, thinking that I had caused it.

Frequently, I would see pets (that had died) walk around my home or sleep on their favorite chair. (This is still common in my life.) My mother tried to tell me that I saw them because I expected to see them. One day I saw my deceased grandmother sitting in a chair at our home, not a place I expected to see her. When I told my mother she stopped telling me I saw things because they met my expectations. During this time, I began to add a line to my prayers (after blessing all of my animals, and all of the animals, and all of the people) "And please don't let me see a ghost."

As a child, my biggest fear was that my father was going to die and leave me.

The death of my father was unexpected. He was young and seemingly in good health, although he did smoke too much. I remember awaking at 12:23 a.m. with my father in the room. He told he had just died of a heart attack. (I was away at the time.) I got up, packed my bag and waited for the phone call which would bring me the news. The entire time this was going on I felt his presence with me, as real in that form as it had ever been in life. When the phone call did come, the information was that he was very ill and had been taken to the hospital. Of course I knew better, because his spirit was beside me giving me the information I needed for the coming days.

When I arrived home, my mother, who had become hysterical, had been sedated, and I was informed that I would have to make the funeral arrangements. Me. I had never been to a funeral in my life. I didn't know the first thing about where to bury my father. North Carolina or Georgia, what type of casket, or worse yet, how much money did we have to do those things?

My father stood by my left shoulder and calmly told me what to do—where to buy a plot, what casket to pick, what music—we argued over the music. I told him that I didn't want to hear his favorite music later in my life and think of his funeral, and other arrangements that he wanted. People who came to our home thought I was either cold or in shock because I showed no grief. How can you show grief when the person who has died is there helping you through a tough situation?

The night of the funeral my father asked me to come sit at the head of the stairs. Here we held our last conversation. "You and your mother are going to be fine. It is time for me to go on. There is an insurance policy I want you to call about that will take care of

you and your mother. I must go now. There are things I have to do."
Then I felt him pull away.

The next day I called about the policy. The company informed
me that he had come in the previous week and taken out a policy,
but he had not come back to sign it. I insisted that they pull the
policy and check.

When they did, it was signed.

My father's death wasn't my first experience with someone who
passed over. In high school I had a magnificent piano teacher who,
for the first time in my life, had awakened the musical talent in me. I
adored this teacher and thought that my whole world depended on
his teaching me forever. Never had I played so well nor enjoyed it as
much as after we met. One evening, after a particularly invigorating
performance, I said to him, "Mr. Young, what would I ever do
without you? I have learned so much and there is so much more I
need to know."

I'll never forget his reply, "I've taught you all I know. All you
need to do is practice."

The next day he committed suicide.

Two weeks later I was scheduled to play in a state music
competition. I refused to go because I could not bring myself to
practice. But my mother and friends encouraged me to go ahead,
saying that Mr. Young would have wanted it that way. The night of
the competition I sat down at the piano, ready to make a complete
fool of myself and not caring. There must have been over a thousand
people in the audience.

Just before I lifted my hands to the keys, I looked to my right,
and there, standing beside the piano was Mr. Young. He smiled and
said, "It's all right. You'll do fine."

And then, one of those magical states happened where the piano
played me. When it was over I was told again and again that people
listening thought it was Mr. Young at the keys. It was. To this day, I
have not played as well, or with such confidence as I did that night.

Mr. Young won the competition that night.

These events were a normal part of my growing up. I didn't
think that they were unusual, or that I had any unusual talents or
skills. I had always believed in fairy tales and magic. Those who
didn't just didn't see "clearly."

THE "REAL WORLD"

I don't remember when I forgot the magic. Somewhere between Psychology 213 and Logic 101, I fell into the "real" world. My life became caught up with parties, the Viet Nam War, graduate school, and a host of other things. My magical world fell by the wayside, as "reality" and the need to be "successful" became my focus.

Interestingly enough, I never had trouble making money or getting the right job at just the right time. In fact, my motto was, "I'm always in the right place at the right time." I didn't realize that this was an affirmation and that I was, indeed, creating my reality . . . and doing a pretty good job of it as long as I didn't give my power away to a nay-sayer. You know the type:

"You'll never get that job, you're too young, inexperienced, female, etc." When I listened to them, and believed what they had to say, I didn't get the job. When I listened to myself, I did.

Throughout my life I always landed in interesting, flexible jobs. Early on I learned that I needed a sense of freedom and autonomy in order to function at my best. It wasn't a conscious thing, but as I continually changed careers: therapist/ researcher/University instructor and litigation analyst for the Attorney General, I knew that I was preparing for something else. Still thinking that in order to prepare you take courses, I was always enrolled in one-degree program or another, usually becoming bored as soon as I got into it. To this day I am amazed I hold any degrees, especially at the Master's level, because my attention span was always so short, and there was a large part of me that whispered,

"This isn't the real knowledge. This is superficial."

While working in the legal field *magic* came back into my life. I began to realize that I wasn't happy. Historically, when I wasn't happy (usually unaware) I would automatically make a change. After making the change, my mood would shift and I would realize I had not been happy doing whatever it was that I was doing. This time I actively realized I wasn't happy. I would sit at my desk and ask, "Why am I not happy? I have a wonderful, exciting position with the Office of the Attorney General— a position that many lawyers would be envious of. I have access to a past and present governor on a first-name basis, as well as to most of the agency heads within the state. I am working on a First Amendment case that is challenging and never dull. I make a good salary. I am married to a handsome, intelligent, kind individual. I have nice clothes, a nice home, car . . . all of the *material* things a person could ask for. What was missing?"

Life, of course was missing. My ego was running the show while my *Spirit* was crying to be set free. All the time, I was asleep and I didn't know it. I would sit in my office and sense an unseen chaos all around me. I couldn't see it, but I knew that it was there.

One day Linda, one of my co-workers, came into my office with a book. "I thought you'd like to look at this," she said.

It was the *I Ching*. Although I had never heard of this book, I quickly became fascinated with it. There, behind the closed doors of my litigation office, I asked about my future and tossed three pennies six times. The first *I Ching* I ever tossed landed on Hexagram Number One with no moving lines. The content of that message, and the power of the *I Ching*, remains with me to this day:

"Creating Power is nothing less than the detonating device in the evolutionary bomb. The time is exceptional in terms of inspiration, energy, and will. The force of this time is the primal directive that propels us into our destinies regardless of what our reasoning or recalcitrant minds may think. What you create now will be the basis and inspiration for what you experience next. As a result of any action you now take, your fate will be sealed. *You may always trace back to the beginning, but there will never be an end to what you are about to set in motion. (I Ching Workbook, R. L. Wing)"*

A chill ran through my body as I read the hexagram. My world shifted, everything felt different. The experimental psychologist in me began to toss the coins again, not for more information but to figure the probability that the three coins would fall in this position six times. Clearly, this hexagram wasn't an accident.

A few days later Linda mentioned that she and four other friends were going to see a "psychic." I had never been to a psychic and doubt that if I had thought about it I would have gone, because I probably would have feared that I would be told something tragic. As luck would have it, one of the four dropped out of their appointment and, on a lark, I decided to go. The last thing I said to my secretary as I left the office was, "She'll probably tell me I'm a psychic." The first thing the psychic said to me when I walked into her presence was, "Why are you here? You're a psychic. You know the answers."

My experience with Noreen Reiner (the psychic) was both mind-blowing and incredible. I couldn't figure out how she knew what she knew . . . was she reading my mind? When I quizzed her on how I should find my psychic ability she replied, "I can't tell you that, that's the journey. You must find it for yourself."

Like most of us, believing that our answers come from books—the thoughts and words of someone else, I began to read. In the three weeks before my First Amendment case was to come to trial, I read twenty-five books. No easy feat when you are working from sunup to midnight preparing for a major legal battle. But read I did, and I still didn't know how I could be psychic. I would say things to people, thinking I was conveying psychic information, and it would turn out to be pure left-brain fiction. I was becoming increasingly frustrated trying to figure out how "psychic awareness" worked.

In spite of my frustration, two "Truths" kept reappearing. Either *there are no accidents or everything is an accident.* And, I discovered a voice in my head that spoke to me, a male voice that seemed somewhat muffled and far away, but a voice that would provide me with accurate information.

Imagination is Real

One morning, just as I was awakening from sleep, frustrated and questioning what to do next, the voice told me to "look around Charlottesville." "Looking" still meant reading, so true to form, I stopped by my favorite bookstore on my way to work. This was typical of my conditioning . . . the answers are in books and there must be another book that I need to read. When I entered the bookstore, I asked Kay, the owner, a question, but before she could answer, the only other person in the store turned and answered the question. I immediately knew that this person had information that I wanted; *she* was why I was in the bookstore that morning, not for a new or better book.

It turned out that this person was a trainer at a place called the Monroe Institute. The institute is an educational and research organization devoted to the premise that "focused consciousness contains all solutions to the questions of human existence. Only through interdisciplinary approaches and research efforts can the understanding of this consciousness be realized."

I immediately went to my office and called the Monroe Institute for information about their program.

"I'd like to come out to see your facility and what you do."

"There's nothing to see," the pleasant voice at the other end of the telephone replied, "and we don't allow people to come through while a program is in progress."

"Then I'll come when there is no program running."

"There is nothing to see."

Taking another tactic, after all, I did work in the legal field: "Can you tell me what you do there?"

"It's hard to explain on the telephone," the voice continued. "It's a process of using sound to balance the hemispheres of the brain." This type of conversation, moving nowhere, continued for about half an hour. Finally, I said, "Send me the application forms."

As I made this request, I wondered how I would find the time and the money to attend a week-long training program doing something I wasn't at all clear about.

Following my newfound knowledge that there are no accidents, I figured that if I wasn't supposed to go, it wouldn't work out. I wouldn't have the money, the trial would go on longer than expected, or I just wouldn't be accepted into the program.

The trial, scheduled to last three weeks (this was the second attempt after many delays and one mistrial), ended three days early. I received a tax refund for the exact amount of the training, and I was accepted into the program.

If anyone had told me that I would spend the next week in a state of primary isolation listening to weird sounds over headphones, I would have said they were crazy. I was just this side of hyperactive, a manic personality, running seven to thirteen miles a day and never sitting still for more than fifteen minutes at any one stretch. I had no idea what I was letting myself in for.

I did go and I did listen to *hemi-sync* several hours a day. I discovered that my "imagination" was real. The pictures in my head gave me accurate information that could be used for messages both about others and myself. Of course, it was not until I was halfway through the program that I figured this out, and not without some help from a co-participant who put his arrowhead necklace in my hand and said, "Tell me what you see."

Immediately I rattled off a series of pictures, in detail and color, which were going through my mind. He said,

"That's me and that's my wife, house, etc."

Unbelievable—images, words and symbols that arose in my mind gave me information I could trust—valid, reliable information.

This same individual encouraged me to take part in the research program at the Institute. The experience and training I received, as an "explorer" was invaluable to my growth in awareness. Nothing can compare with being in a sensory-deprivation booth, listening to soothing sounds coming through headphones, and having two very well trained experts at the other end ask me questions about myself, the Universe, and life in general.

It was also through my training at the Institute that I began to learn that we do know when someone else thinks of us, we can "throw" energy wherever we desire, and that healing and communication are possible using this same form of energy.

You Are More than Your Physical Body

The entire time I was at the Monroe Institute training program I was trying to decide if I thought there was such a thing as an "out-of-body" experience or if it was remote viewing. While I did have some interesting experiences in the form of feeling my hands and arms lift out of my body, I couldn't say I knew what an OBE (Out-of-Body Experience) was. As would often happen when I asked a heart-felt question, the *powers that be* gave such a detailed answer I couldn't deny its validity.

Noreen was holding a séance, and I went with friends. Not being in touch with modern-day channeling, I thought I could call in my father and ask him why I was afraid to be psychic? Was there something I feared?

The evening was set with eleven other people, candles, and a Doberman for good measure. Noreen asked that we all relax, a state very easy for me to accomplish, while she drew in her sources, but for some reason, she was unable to channel that evening.

Now I understand that I was drawing her energy. Following a technique that I learned at Monroe, when Noreen instructed us to relax, I had counted myself into a deeply relaxed state, and when I did, I pulled in large amounts of Universal energy, including the energy around her.

After she was unable to get into trance, Noreen decided to go around the room and tell the participants what guilt they brought into this life. Perhaps this wasn't the best thing to do, but on the other hand, it became very significant or me.

Looking at me, Noreen began to talk about my fingers. (I am very sensitive about my fingers.) I thought it was because I play the piano and was constantly told as a child to protect my hands). She said, "You were tortured. Your fingers were broken back and then chopped off!"

She had barely finished speaking when my surroundings changed. Instead being a brown-eyed brunette, I had red hair and green eyes. Instead of sitting in a chair, I was tied to a stake and the fire was burning my legs. I was smothering. "It's not fair! It's not fair!" I screamed. The other members of the séance had turned into a group of people surrounding me, watching me burn. (Later, one man told me he thought he lit the fire.)

Noreen jumped up, ran over to where I was and waved her hands over me. I remember thinking, "This isn't helping," followed by, "Is it possible for a soul to die in the same way twice?" As I burned, it seemed I was floating up, out of my body.

In the middle of this drama, a woman in the room began to have an epileptic seizure. My thoughts left my "burning" to the thought," I can heal her." I went to her, held her head in my hands, and her seizure stopped. At this point I began to sense a lot of negative energy in the room, and I found myself arguing about this with Noreen, who tried to persuade me that the energy wasn't negative. By now, I knew I had to get out of there, so I went out, sat on her porch, put my feet and hands on the ground and rested my head on my knees. It was raining and the warm, spring rain felt good to my traumatized body.

Later in the evening I became worried about Sharon, a young girl who was still in the séance. Knowing that she was afraid, I felt that I should go help her with her fears. Standing up, I went to the front door, noticed the handle of the door, and went into the foyer. The Doberman was there, but seemed to be ignoring me. (This was highly unusual for this very protective dog.)

Someone opened the door to the room where the séance was being held, so I moved quickly across the room to Sharon. I wondered why they had turned up the lights and why the Doberman took such a circuitous route to reach the same place in the room as me.

Taking Sharon's hands in mine, I told her she was safe, just to ignore Noreen and what was going on. I heard Noreen say, "Your fears have called the spirits," as she started to move over to us. I backed away and, it would seem, returned to the porch.

The next thing I knew, my two friends were shaking me, asking if I was all right. I couldn't stand up. They carried me to their car and then up to my apartment and put me to bed. In the middle of the night I woke up and realized that I was still burning. My thought was, "Oh, no! You haven't counted yourself back to consciousness after relaxing at the beginning of the séance!" Taking a deep breath, I counted back to one and the burning sensation stopped.

The next day my friends told the following story. Once I left the room I did not return. After about an hour had passed Noreen said, "There's a spirit at the door. Let the spirit in." Someone opened the door and my friends saw a grey mass float across the room.

When we questioned Sharon, whose eyes had been tightly shut because of her fear, she said, "Yes, Winter, you came to me and comforted me. You held my hands and I felt much calmer with you than I did with the psychic. I wish you hadn't left!"

Not only had I been out-of-body, but also my "higher self" had set me up in such a fashion that I couldn't deny what had taken place. How many individuals have eleven other people who can verify that they have moved around without any physical form?

The next evening, I realized that it is probably harder to stay in your body than it is to get out of it. I decided to practice backing out by a method I had been taught at the Monroe Institute. I found it quite easy to back out, and as I stood by my bed, preparing to go somewhere, I was suddenly seized on the arms by four strong pinching hands. "Um," I thought. "Guess I'll stay home tonight." There have been other times I have suddenly found myself across a room staring back at my physical form and watching myself talking. On one such occasion, a male friend of mine had become, perhaps, a little too friendly. Not wanting to rebuff him, and wanting to maintain our friendship, I chose to move from the sofa where we were sitting and walk across the room. It was after I turned back to speak to him that I realized my physical body was still on the sofa. The interesting thing was that he knew I had left my body on that occasion and later called my attention to the fact.

Now, like most individuals who have discovered their OBE's, I work to consciously know when I am out. I had two instances of being out with friends happen during the same week. During the first instance one of my friends floated through the door of my bedroom and complained that her husband had said something to her that she didn't like. The second instance occurred a few days later, when I was visiting a good friend that I had not seen for several months. I was looking forward to having a glass of wine with him and catching up on his life as a resident. As luck would have it, when I arrived for the visit he had the worst cold he had ever had in his life. We had a quick dinner and he promptly went to bed.

During the night he floated through the wall and lay beside me. I don't remember what was said, but the next morning I awoke with a wonderful sense of peace and the knowledge that we had been able to converse after all.

At first, I was upset that both of my friends had apparently been able to leave their bodies so easily while I was still in mine. Later I realized that I had to have been out of my body in order to see them.

Masters

One sunny afternoon I was in my kitchen, calmly washing dishes, when I felt the hair on my neck stand up. Something was behind me. Turning to face the refrigerator, I first saw glitter all around the base of the refrigerator and then, very slowly, an eight-foot-tall being, with long grey robes, begin to take shape. No, I didn't say, "Oh, what a wonderful being you are," but instead I waved a shaky hand and said, "Not now!" The being quickly went away. This episode, more than ever, made me question the out-of-body state. Was this a guardian, or a friend coming to visit without form?

Just because one sends away an apparition in a long grey robe doesn't mean that they won't return. I think my guardians, or masters, must have decided, "OK, so she doesn't want to see us . . . we'll just talk to her." And **talk** they did. I kept hearing, "Don't drink."

I would argue, "I've been a therapist in an addiction treatment center, I know how much is too much, and I only drink one glass of wine or one bottle of Heineken a day. That isn't addiction." Still, the message would come, "Don't drink." Still, I would argue.

One night I had a dream, a dream that would make Dickens's *Christmas Carol* look like a scene from *Bambi.* In the dream two "Spirits" stood on either side of me and walked me through my life, beginning in the doctor's office. No matter where they took me, I couldn't keep my eyes open, especially my left eye, which in ancient literature is the eye to the soul.

We ended up in front of the elevators of a very tall building. These elevators went to two floors: two and six. (Remember Ram Dass and the channels that we operate on? Channel one is our physical body. Channel two, our personality. Channel three, new age: Libra, Pisces rising. Channel four, we look into a mirror and there is a multitude of reflections looking back at us. Channel five, we look at another individual and that same someone is looking back at us, and Channel six: the nothingness from which we come.) This elevator only went to floor two (personality) and six (the ultimate). I couldn't make it to floor two because I was asleep.

On waking the next morning, I said, "All right, I won't drink. But you had better show me something." I was always trying to make deals, and my guardians let me think that I was striking deals with the Universe.

Fast forward to a dinner party that I was hosting the following weekend. While sitting at the dinner table listening to a conversation about medical insurance, zoning problems, and which diamond necklace to purchase, I realized I was bored. A nice glass of wine would be perfect. In fact, I resented the fact that these individuals were drinking my wine while I was sitting there wishing for a way to escape. All of a sudden my attention was drawn out of my dining room and I saw the gray-robed apparition cross the hall. "Oh, my God, this is what I've been missing!" Later, I realized I would see the shadow of this being on the walls and in other places where there was nothing else that could make the shadow.

It was during this same period of initial psychic awareness that my inner voice kept pulling me to Georgia, the home of my father. For some strange reason I felt the need to find the "Native American" in our family. I was certain that somewhere along the line someone had been married to a Native American.

Not only did my cousins looked like full-blooded Cherokees, when my father moved to North Carolina, he was a good friend with Chief Walking Stick, Chief of the Eastern Band of the Cherokee.

It has been said that once you step out onto the path of seeking your spiritual self you travel a lot, to distant and near places, and you meet the most interesting individuals. I thought of this as I took three days' leave from work and stepped onto a plane headed for a place I had not visited in seventeen years. I arrived to find wonderful, friendly cousins, but only one who would admit to the fact that she thought she had heard my grandmother speak of an "Indian" in the family.

Searching for my history, I discovered that there was a well-maintained Native American burial ground on the family property. My only family connection to the genetic lineage of my father's family, his eldest sister, for reasons of her own, swore that there were no Native Americans in the family despite her three children's black, straight hair, high cheekbones, and dark eyes.

While my visit did not turn up any factual evidence of a Native American heritage, I did discover that the family came from Pike County, Louisiana (Cajun?), and I heard the old ghost stories about the family home which I had heard as a child.

For my return to Virginia, I had booked the same flight as I had coming down. It made one brief stop in North Carolina and I had remained on the airplane.

As I sat on the plane waiting to take off, I heard the voice say, "You're on the wrong plane."

"I'm not on the wrong plane. They checked my ticket; this is the same flight I took down. I am on the right plane."

"You're on the wrong plane."

The door closed and we prepared for take off.

There were only six of us on the plane, as it was midweek and not many people travel from Augusta to Virginia midweek. All at once I looked up to see the most handsome man standing by my seat smiling at me. I immediately felt that I was looking at a physician, but I couldn't be certain of his nationality. Perhaps he was from India? He had dark hair, deep blue, intense eyes and a wonderful smile. "Pardon me miss, but you are sitting in my seat."

"No, I'm certain I'm in the correct seat." Actually, what difference would it make? The plane has lots of empty seats, I thought. Just to satisfy him I pulled out my ticket. I *was* on the wrong plane and I just had enough time to get off! Otherwise I would have ended up much further north than was my intention. As I started to get off the plane, I turned to tell the man that I was in his seat and he could move. He wasn't on the plane. The other original five people were still on the airplane and that was *all* that were there. My mysterious physician was nowhere to be seen.

When I began trying to hear my inner voice, I had a lot of help. It was clear I didn't pay attention very well! My contact with my inner guidance (or outer guidance, as the case may be) became subtler as I learned to listen. The dramatic events became less and less frequent, the inner voice more prominent. For instance, one morning I had finished a long jog and was getting ready to shower before heading to a seminar I was teaching. My husband had requested that I drop off some blueprints for him that morning, as he had out of-town business. I had forty-five minutes to clean up, deliver the blueprints and get to my seminar location. I jumped into my car, sweaty and smelly, and raced down the street to the office of the architect. I was half-way to my destination when I realized, "You have locked yourself out of the house." Which door is open? None. Which window is open? No window. Who else has a key? No one within calling distance. Which window/door do I break to get in?" (All of this was my left brain seeking rational, methodical ways to get into a locked house). It was at this point the voice in my head said, "If you turn right now you'll run into John (my husband). John had left two hours earlier to go to another city. How could I turn right in the middle of downtown Norfolk, Virginia, and meet him?

I didn't question this information. I turned right, drove a few blocks, and sure enough, I ran into John as he was driving down the street. He had been delayed in leaving town.

A similar experience happened when, as was usually the case, I raced out of my home on the way to another city. I reached the end of my driveway and realized I did not have any type of coat. So what? Virginia had been having a wonderful warm spell in the middle of February. The temperature had been and was predicted to continue to be in the eighties for the next few days. When I realized I didn't have a coat, I thought that a raincoat would be the most practical coat for the occasion. I raced back into the house, reached into the closet and pulled out . . . my down parka! I thought, "This is crazy. It's eighty degrees, I am dressed in white linen, the temperature is going to stay in the eighties and I am taking a down parka with me!" But I didn't put it back. I took it to my destination, which was also quite warm— sweater weather at night—and awoke the next morning to an unpredicted and unexpected snow storm. The down parka was the only warm thing I had with me. This was *lucky* for me because I became stranded and had to walk a mile in the snow.

You've Got To Decide Which Way You Are Going To Go.

Even though many wonderful, mystical things were happening to me, I was busy furthering my career in the public sector and politics in general. It was an interesting combination, because during the day I would be working with politicians who tried to manipulate the minds of the public, and at night I would be out telling the public to control their own minds, lives, and destinies.

It was while I was attending a political function that a friend came up and said, "You'll want to meet my neighbor. She's a psychic." I thought, "The last thing I need to meet is another psychic. But when he said "She's eighty years old," I realized I *did* want to meet her. I was sure she had a lot to share.

When I called to make my appointment for a reading, she asked me what I did, and I told her that I was involved in politics but that I was psychic and I enjoyed the mystical side of life.

"You've got to decide which way you are going to go," she said. Those wise words were exactly what I needed to hear. I didn't need a reading to tell me I was standing between two worlds, or that change was taking place in my life. I needed a push from someone who would say,

"You have to make a choice. Step out, take a risk, and see what happens. It won't be dull!"

The next day I set in motion the necessary details to form my own business. I told those I was working with that I wouldn't be taking on any new contracts, that I was going to start consulting in the business world. At this point in time I thought my consulting would be very traditional, based on the knowledge I had acquired both academically and experientially. But what I thought I was going to consult about and what actually came out of my mouth were two different things.

I would go into a setting and say what I thought to be outrageous things about how the mind worked and how we should view life. The amazing thing was that the business community accepted what I said. Certainly something else was helping me in my endeavors . . . something with much more power than I could imagine.

My biggest fear in teaching whole brain thinking was the fact that I would have to learn to relax large groups of people in order to show them how their right hemisphere worked. I had never been comfortable trying to relax anyone, even one person in a private therapy session. How could I possibly think I could relax a large audience, especially one made up of businessmen?

The first workshop I conducted was at a local University and was filled with businessmen and women. I was doing fine until it came time for the relaxation exercise, when my old fears started to rise. It was then that an interesting thing took place. As I dimmed the lights and turned on the music, I sensed an energy come into the room and move behind the audience. When this energy reached my left side I began the exercise. I was extremely calm. It was as though someone else was leading the participants exactly where they were supposed to go. After the exercise, I had one woman tell me that she had started to get a migraine, but when I started to talk she felt the tension leave and the headache go away. Everyone in the audience seemed to go to a state of complete relaxation. And no one was more amazed than I.

This type of help has become very normal during the last two years. I always know that this energy will come and lead participants gently into their own state of relaxation. I always know that if I am giving a talk to a specific group of individuals, whether they be architects or physicians, the energy will flow through me to speak specifically to that audience. Data and facts that I do not know consciously, information that is pertinent to the situation at hand, will come forth. All I need to do is, "show up, tell the truth, and not be attached to the outcome." (Angeles Arrien)

Even as I sit and write this book I know that things are included that I would not, consciously, have thought to include.

Yosemite Sam

After my week-long retreat at Monroe I began to psychically "read" anyone who was willing. Through practice I learned the difference between *my* symbology and the symbology that belonged to the individual I was reading. I also began to trust the information I was receiving. If you can verify the answers you receive as soon as possible, you build confidence in your process.

While all my spare time went to "reading" the world, I continued to return to Monroe to be an explorer in their lab. Part of the work was remote viewing experiments (remote viewing is the ability to see what is happening at a time and place one has never visited). One day, after being given a series of coordinates and asked to "see" what was there, I saw "Sam the Pirate," complete with red mustache and sword.

Sam began to tell me information about my monitor who was in another room. Essentially, he began to go through her body from head to toe, concluding with,

"And this is what she must do if she is to get better." After I came out of the session, I discovered that this information, at least the part that talked about her physical ailments, was correct. She said she could try the remedies he suggested. They made sense to her.

It was later in one of these sessions that I was told I was to work with the healers of the planet. I thought that someone "upstairs" had to be off. What physician did I know that would work with a psychic—one who had absolutely no medical background, or any interest in getting medical experience?

Eight months later I attended a professional meeting and sat next to a gentleman who introduced himself as a biochemist. It turned out that he was also a physician and is today the primary physician with whom I work. The group of physicians I work with has grown rapidly in number and ranges from internists and surgeons to psychiatrists.

The biochemist, Al, was interested in researching this phenomenon. What type of information did I receive? Was it accurate, and just as importantly, was it useful?

We set up a project to find out. Several times a week we would "scan" the body of someone who had some type of physical ailment or disease. Often a subject would come back to us to "thank" us for the healing. We would say "Thank you," all the while thinking that we weren't healing, we were just scanning the body for useful and helpful information.

One of our readings was for a young woman with temporal lobe epilepsy. After we gave her neuro-psychologist the information she (the patient) wanted to meet with me. I couldn't imagine why. I knew I had said all that there was to say, but I agreed to meet with her at the home of Al and to have her neuro-psychologist in attendance. When I met her I saw that she had several serious problems, including a hand that was turning inward and curling up and a speech problem. I remember wondering just what I was supposed to do when I heard, "Heal her."

"You don't understand. I do body scanning and evaluations. I don't *do* healing. Besides, look at her. Her problems are very noticeable. Couldn't you give me someone easy to start with?"

"Heal HER!"

I moved over to the sofa and took her twisted hand in my own. I could feel the energy that she was turning inward on herself.

"Marsha, you are doing this to your body and you have to take control of this energy. No one else can do it for you. You are going to start by healing your hand." I then proceeded to tell her about a past life where she was a Chinese man who had let his nails grow through his hand in order that he might have control over his life.

"Oh, my gosh!" she cried out. "That is the life I saw when I first underwent hypnosis!" She finished the story that I had begun. The energy in the room changed and I felt a oneness with her, unlike anything I had ever experienced.

Marsha left, her hand still twisted and her speech still slurred. Two weeks later I received a telephone call from Al: "I've got to tell you about Marsha. She was putting a splint on her hand every night in order to keep it from retracting more. She forgot to put the splint on and woke up to find her hand was normal. Not only that, but she doesn't have a speech problem anymore."

One of my most interesting "healing" experiences came when I was with my friend Michael Hutchison (author of *Megabrain*) in New York City. Michael had not been feeling well for several months, and as we strolled around Central Park, I had this strong feeling that I wanted to "heal" him. "Michael, I am going to make you one of the most unusual propositions you may ever receive. I want you to come back to where I am staying so that I can heal you."

Michael is truly some type of brother-like, soul connection. I have had some of my most incredible psychic experiences with him, and I have seen past lives where he was my brother and took care of me. In this life I think it is my turn to take care of him. We returned to the apartment where I was staying. I remember thinking, "Okay, now what are you going to do? This was your idea, after all."

I asked Michael to lie down. Placing my hand on his liver I thought," I'll imagine I am running healing white light here and maybe I'll know what to do next." All at once I felt as if someone or something had switched on the power, and current raced through my body with an intensity I had never, ever felt. I couldn't move my hand, and I knew that if it didn't stop soon, I would be so energized I wouldn't be able to sleep, or be able to conduct a workshop the next day.

A loud voice boomed, "That's enough!" As if a lever was pulled, the white light shut off. Immediately, I fell into a lucid dreamlike state where Michael and I were traveling in a car with two dogs. When I woke up, Michael had been aware of the everything, including the voice that said, "That's enough!" and the dream. He had the same dream, and in his dream he even named the dogs, which we had picked up by the road, one of which was "Hug A Door." A few days later, when Michael went to see his physician, he was pronounced perfectly healthy.

My only other time of becoming so immersed with this light or energy occurred several years ago at the Omega. Starhawk was leading a workshop, asking us to imagine ourselves as trees. We were, supposedly, bringing the Universal energy from the ground up into our bodies for "grounding." I can't tell you that I believed in that sort of thing. This was one of those instances where it was cold and rainy, and my mind was on how cold I was. I wanted to get to a warmer space, and do something, anything but stand outside in the cold. As I stood in a circle of about twenty individuals, I suddenly became aware that the soles of my feet were heating up. I felt the heat move up my legs, and as it did so, everything around me turned *golden*.

As the heat (or energy) moved up my body, the brightness of the golden color increased and I became physically hot. In fact, I was sweating. Soon, I was unable to see the other people in the circle. All I could see was this very bright, golden light. I remember thinking that I had to leave the circle in one way or another. Either I would physically break the chain (we were holding hands) and leave, or I was going to pass out. Just at the point where I felt that I could no longer stand the intensity of the heat and the light, Starhawk said, "Now bend down to the ground and run the energy back to the source from which it came." As I bent down I saw a blade of grass that appeared to have been magnified several million times. The intricate workings of the fiber stood out, and I could see with great clarity the water droplets on its surface. As soon as I put my head to the ground the light disappeared and the grass blade returned to a normal size.

This was my first conscious, *Satori* experience. (*Satori*, roughly translated means a flash of sudden awareness. It comes in a split

second, when you just *know* something that you didn't know before.)
I have since learned that it is this same golden light that heals, that
creates, that helps us be more than our physical bodies. Al and I
have witnessed many other healing successes and many attempts
at healing where nothing happened. A *Course in Miracles* says,
"Miracles are natural. It is when they do not occur that something
has gone wrong." We both know that it's up to the individual soul
to heal its body. I can point out what is causing the situation, tell
the person several ways to remedy the situation (which may, in fact,
include very traditional medical approaches), but only that soul can
heal itself. I also know that added energy can help, e.g., sending
white light, visualizing them well, or praying for them.

In the chapters that follow, I share some of my thoughts on how
intuition can be utilized in all aspects of our lives, from personal
to business, creativity to health. Antoine de Exupery once wrote, It
is only with the heart that one can see rightly; what is essential is
invisible to the eye. Let us begin to see rightly.

PART TWO

Messages from Everywhere

It is only with the heart that one can see rightly, what is essential is invisible to the eye.

—Antoine De Saint-Exupery, *The Little Prince*

CHAPTER ONE

Types of Intuition

Carl Jung once related a story about a conversation with Ochwiay Bianco, then chief of the Pueblo Indians. When asked, Bianco told Jung that his opinion of the white man was not very high because they always seem upset, restless, and looking for something. The result of this is their faces are wrinkled. Not only that, they must be crazy because they think with their heads and it is well known that only crazy people do that. "How do you think?" Jung asked. "Naturally," Bianco replied, "with my heart."

We have the answers: the heart always brings them to us. It is the questions that are difficult. We don't know what we want to know, and we don't know how to ask the question in order to get the answer. In truth, the answers are always right before our nose, ever present.

Gertrude Stein was asked, as she was on her deathbed, if she had found the answers to her questions. "More importantly," she replied, "What is the question?"

We all carry questions around with us, some not fully formulated, many not in our conscious awareness. You may not be happy with your present job, relationship, living environment, etc. Your unhappiness is your heart telling you that you need to make a change. It is time to move on, to grow. All too often we see the door open and realize it represents an answer to an unasked question.

Your heart, or intuition, imagination, creativity, sixth sense, are all the same thing. We just use different names according to the environment we are in. Scientists call it the right hemisphere, Carl Jung called it the "collective unconscious," and Rupert Sheldrake, a present day biologist, calls it "Morphogenetic Resonance."

Intuition is the inner voice, the flow of the Universe, energy, the Oversoul, the Higher Self, the *I Am* presence—in short, it's the sum total of all that we are, all that we can become.

Much has been written on intuition, what it is and what it is not. Discussions abound on whether it exists or doesn't exist. However, despite the many words, clearly there is enough evidence that something exists which provides us information which we have no logical way of knowing, information which, if we act upon it, could be useful and helpful—not only in our everyday lives, but toward our spiritual growth as well.

When I began my workshops, I concentrated on helping students tap into their psychic/intuitive abilities. Since then, my focus has been to introduce individuals to the "Universal Energy," the flow of the Universe. If we can learn to be in that flow life goes along much more smoothly. It isn't such an effort and battle just to live from day to day. There is a wonderful rhythmic order to things.

Often I will interchange the word *psychic* with *intuition* because they come from the same source. Psychic comes from the Greek word "psyche," meaning soul or spirit. The original definition of a psychiatrist was one who heals the soul, and of psychologist, one who studies the soul. It's time we took the voodoo and mystery out of these words and returned to their original meanings. Every human is "psychic," that is, we are all spirit.

There are various ways in which we hear "spirit" or receive psychic or intuitive information, the first of these being "physical." Attuned, the physical body is one of the most important means of receiving information that is not apparent. For instance, if you get a headache each time you go to work or when you meet a particular person, it is your body telling you that something is out of sync. Either your work is too stressful and you are creating your own headache in the first example or, in the second instance, the person you are in contact with has a headache, and *you* feel it!

The second type of intuition is "emotional." An example of this would be when you meet an individual who is highly praised by mutual friends, and you aren't able to share those feelings. Until the reasons become apparent, you begin to doubt your own feelings. But when they do, you realize you knew it all the time.

The third type of intuition is "mental" and can be received via dreams or the feeling of *déjà vu*, that you have been somewhere before. And it's quite possible that you have, in a dream, visited the very site you found yourself in—years later. Also, using the mental facilities, some people are able to get mental pictures as answers to their intuitive questions.

Since reception of intuitive senses varies from individual to individual, it is important to know how you receive your answers. Some people see pictures, others hear music or voices, and still others just have thoughts pop into their minds—all seemingly from nowhere.

Others sense information in their bodies, perhaps they experience a chill when something that is said rings true or is important for them to remember.

I get a pressure on my back if I am checking someone for allergies, or I may actually sneeze if the person is allergic to the substance I am scanning. I also receive chills, and at times my right ear closes if something is being said that I need to pay attention to.

The more we pay attention to our body, the more we can evaluate and use the information which we receive.

It is important to ask clear questions, one at a time. Several questions at once will bring several answers, all at the same time!

Then be prepared to see, hear, feel, or experience the answers in the way that your soul speaks to you. When you receive an answer to a question, and we receive answers to our questions all of the time, take time to check the answer. Take it to your heart, how does it feel there? Remember, often we have been carrying a question around with us for months, not realizing that we were asking anything at all. When the answer hits, we have the eureka effect— we know what the question was!

QUESTIONS

Q: How can I tell the difference between "me" and my intuition?

A: Your intuition speaks softly and repeatedly. It isn't judgmental and it doesn't lose patience with giving you the answer again and again, and again.

Sometimes it is just a feeling of strong love or uneasiness. Our "chattering mind," uses a lot of shoulds and ought's when it speaks. It is that part of you that tries to make you feel guilty. Guilt is optional, not something we have to do or be.

Q: More than anything else I would like to be psychic, to know the future and to be able to "read" others. How can I?

A: We all know our future because we are busy creating it. Once we become aware of this fact we can work to create what we want and not become engrossed with worrying about what we don't want. As far as being able to "read" others, we do that on a daily basis as well. There are many situations we find ourselves in where we "know" what is taking place but are not at liberty to say what we think or feel.

Once you discover that you do know these things, they aren't nearly as interesting. You realize that everyone is alike, on the same path, with the same problems. Being psychic isn't the end result of getting in touch with our intuition. Psychic is only the glitter, there to entice us to see more, lots more. We are trying to get in touch with *Spirit* in any way we can, that's what is important.

Q: My intuitive answers seem to come from the center of my chest. When I get a certain feeling there, do I know that a truth is being said or I should follow my feelings?

A: This is your heart bringing you an answer. Know that when your heart brings you an answer, you should follow it. It may be that you find it going in two directions, but then you can go in two directions also. It is more important to open up and experience the knowledge the heart brings, always to do with love, unconditional love, than to shut down and limit life. If you don't follow your heart and stay only in your head, you will have less of an emotional response. But then you have to ask yourself, are you making the most of this life if you avoid your feelings and following where your heart leads?

MEDITATION

Sit or lie in a comfortable position with your clothing loose and your shoes off. Be aware of your breath. Does it go deeply into your stomach or does it stop in your chest? Close your eyes and breathe deeply, making sure you take your air all the way down to your lower stomach—about three inches below the navel—the *d'en tien*, as the Chinese call it. After you have watched your breath for a few minutes, begin to notice the thoughts that pop into your head, the pictures that come up, or any other "mental" activity that may be going on.

Observe any feeling that you have *on* your body. Do you have any unusual tingling sensations? Is there any pain or discomfort? Think of someone you don't like.

How does your body respond? Do you notice a reaction any particular place on your body? Now think of someone you love or care for. How does your body feel now?

Continue to think of love, letting it flow out into the Universal all around you and to all of life. Open your eyes and come back to the present.

EXERCISE

Put on a tape or record of music that has no particular melody, just flowing melody, such as any songs by Deuter or any music you feel is relaxing. Relax and watch the pictures, images, feelings, thoughts, words, or symbols that appear in your mind. Does the music create a picture, a story, or remind you of something in the past? Continue to listen to the music, paying attention to how it affects your physical body as you listen. When the music is over, write down what you saw or felt, along with any other information which came to you during the exercise.

What if you slept?
And what if in your sleep, you dreamed?
And what if in your dream you went to heaven and there plucked a strange and beautiful flower? And what if, when you awoke, you had the flower in your hand? Ah! What then?

—Samuel Taylor Coleridge

CHAPTER TWO

Dreams

In *Dream Game*, Ann Faraday calls dreams "thoughts from the heart." Because I view intuition as information that comes from the heart which you must take back to the heart in order to clarify, I like the concept that dreams also come from the heart. If we view our unconscious as information that comes from our heart, it doesn't become fearful, but rather positive wisdom that helps us move forward in life.

For many years' psychologists have tried to fit dreams and the dreamer into a specific mold, which never works. Dreams and their interpretations are as individualistic as the dreamer himself. A more contemporary view of dreams is to have the dreamers make their own interpretation of their dream and to work out the symbology their mind has given to them.

Your mind can only use the symbols and words you are most familiar with, in order to give you a message either about yourself or your life situation. Water in your dreams may not mean the same thing as water in someone else's dream, even though water tends to be a universal symbol for the unconscious and spiritual part of you.

Symbols can be tricky, and you may need to work with your dream over a few days in order to interpret it to your satisfaction. A snake, for example, can mean anything from real snakes in your environment (human or otherwise) to the world of medicine and healing.

An example of a more Universal symbol would be a chair. If you are trying to discover the symbology behind the chair, become the chair itself and speak. "I am a chair; people sit on me without any regard for my feelings. I am just a piece of furniture, one that is easily overlooked except when someone wants to use me."

While it may seem as if there are endless possibilities, when you begin recording your dreams and narrowing down your options to specific parameters, the picture gradually comes into focus. These revealing "sign posts" can be used to improve the way you feel about something, hence to improve your life.

QUESTIONS

The following are some of the most common questions I hear concerning dreams:

Q: Why do we dream?

A: Technically, scientists don't know the answer to that. It is known that our REM (rapid eye movement) or dream state is the most important part of our total sleep time. We always dream. On a more personal basis, we dream to get in touch with our heart, our unconscious. Dreams come to tell us something that we don't know about either our personal life, environment or future. If your dream appears to bring you obvious information, look deeper. There is no need to spend your dream state being told that of which you are already aware.

Q: Why can't I remember my dreams?

A: You have no interest in recalling them. When you decide that you would like to know what is going on in that part of your life, you will send a message to your unconscious mind to begin to help you remember your dreams. Once you have done this, place a pencil and paper or a tape recorder by your bedside. This will serve as a reminder that you are going to recall your dreams and will be writing or telling about them in some manner.

Q: I only remember parts of my dreams, other parts are vague.

A: Upon arising, write down what you do remember and make up the rest. Put down how the dream felt and what you think it was concerning. After this you will find that you will begin to remember a few more details. The habit of recording your dreams will help you to remember them. When you begin to work with your dreams, begin looking for symbols that are consistent and make sense to you. At the end of recording the dream, make a note on what you intend to do about the problem which surfaced in the dream.

Q: There are "dream groups" in which individuals work to help clarify the dreams of others. Are groups useful?

A: Edgar Cayce said that only the dreamer knows the correct meaning of their dream, and it is correct only when it makes sense to them and feels right. The dream should be consistent with other dreams and move the dreamer forward in life. I think that the dreamer should first make his interpretation of the dream, and then ask others for their insights if need be, but to go to a group solely for the purpose of having them make the interpretation allows the dreamer to become lazy in processing his inner work.

Q: What if after working very hard on a dream I still don't understand it?

A: Ask your higher consciousness for a clarification dream. This is a dream that brings you the same answer in a different way. You can also ask for verification on the way that you interpreted the dream.

Q: Are all dreams the same?

A: Dreams can be classified according to the information which they provide or the feeling they invoke.

Precognitive dreams are dreams which contain information on future events. You may or may not be able to act upon this information and it may or may not concern you. It is possible for a precognitive dream to give you information about someone you barely know.

Symbolic, possibly the most common type of dream, which serves to bring us information from our unconscious to help us move forward.

Lucid, or out-of-body dreams, where the dreamer knows he is dreaming. In the lucid state the dreamer has the option of flying, changing the plot, going to see anyone he desires or to any place he thinks about. Dreams about flying or some mode of transportation should serve as an alert to the dreamer that he has been out of body.

Q: I frequently dream of my husband. Am I really dreaming about him or am I dreaming about the male part of myself?

A: Because you know your husband, the dream is probably telling you something about him or your relationship to him. When you dream of someone you know, the dream is actually about them. When you dream of a stranger you must look to interpret if the stranger is a part of you of which you are not aware, an actual person you might meet in the future, or something else entirely. If, for example, you dream of a "John Hurt," ask yourself if you actually know a John Hurt. If there is no one in your life with the name of Hurt, ask if someone is hurting you or if you are hurting someone else by your actions. Remember that dreams come to tell us what we don't consciously know, not what we are aware of.

Q: How do I learn to have an out-of-body experience?

A: Every one of us travels during our sleep. The trick is to remember that we traveled or to be aware (lucid) at the time we are traveling. Ask your higher self to make you aware of when you travel. It may take a few days or weeks before you begin to be knowledgeable about this state, and you may find that you are aware for only a few minutes, that you only got a passing glimpse of your out-of-body state. As you become more aware of what it feels like to be "out," you can consciously work to be more aware of "getting out," of freeing your astral body from your physical body.

Q: Are there specifics to be included when recording dreams?

A: Yes. Try seeing your dream as a "dream play" and write your notes accordingly. This will help you begin to interpret your dreams more fully and enhance your enjoyment of writing them down.

Consider:

The setting or time and place of the dream and its relevance to the present. Did the dream take place during the Civil War, and did you find yourself in a Confederate hospital? Do you work in the medical profession now? Are you trying, or not trying, to be civil to someone . . . possibly a confederate?

The plot or trigger points. Do you find you are unable to complete a specific task no matter how many times you try? Is the confederate undermining you in some fashion?

The scene. Where does this scene fit in the rest of your dreams, your life? Does the scene change?

Cast of characters. Are they people that you know, love, or are they strangers? How do they relate to you in this scene?

The feeling. How does this dream leave you feeling? After you interpret the dream, you should feel uplifted with new insight. If you don't then you have misinterpreted the dream. Dreams don't come to us to make us unhappy; they come to give us clarity.

Word play. For example, a person named "Rob" could suggest the act of robbing someone or taking something that doesn't belong to you, and the word "gilded" could be masking the word "guilt."

The peak of the dream, the incident when the plot matures and reaches its climax. This is the opportunity for the characters to separate themselves from the plot, and the dreamer has the opportunity to see how they react in his "real" life.

Although most people have a favorite or an outstanding dream, my favorite is not one I dreamed myself. It came to me by way of a telephone call from a distant friend who had dreamed of me the night before. I had a vague recollection of having thought (dreamed?) of him as well. He explained the dream and then named the other leading character. It was, indeed, someone I knew. But what made the dream so outstanding was the fact that this long and distant friend had never heard of the other person in the dream prior to having the dream.

MEDITATION

Relax in bed with the lights off. Scan your mind and release any worries or thoughts from the day that seem to be hanging on. This can be done by visualizing the problem, seeing it with a perfect ending, surrounding it with a pink bubble, and releasing it to the Universe. (See Chapter 10, "Visualization.")

Select an area of your life to which you would like an answer. Frame the question as simply and as clearly as you can, e.g. "Should I consider the new job that is opening at work?" Ask your heart to bring you an answer. Be sure that you have a note pad and pencil next to your bed in order to record your dreams when you awaken.

During the day, ask yourself if you are dreaming. According to Stephen LeBerge *(Lucid Dreaming),* this will help you be aware of when you are dreaming at night and make it easier for you to have a lucid dream.

Actively create a dream. Write down a dream that you would like to have occur. Remember to put it in color and add all of the details you would like to see happen, including people, places and things. When you have finished recording the dream, fold the paper toward you three times and place it in a safe, loving space. Wait, and see what happens.

There is a vitality, a life force, a quickening that is translated through you into action, and there is only one of you in all time. This expression is unique, and if you block it, it will never exist through any other medium; and be lost. The world will not have it.

It is not your business to determine how good it is, not how it compares with other expression. It is your business to keep it yours clearly and directly, to keep the channel open. You have to keep open and aware directly to the urges that motivate you. Keep the channel open.

No artist is pleased. There is no satisfaction whatever at any time. There is only a queer, divine dissatisfaction, a blessed unrest that keeps us marching and makes us more alive than the others.

—Martha Graham

CHAPTER THREE

Life/Career

What shall I do with the rest of my life is probably one of the most common questions put to a psychic. Ironically, the high school or college graduate usually does not ask this question, but rather individuals reaching their mid-thirties or beyond, ready to take a hard look at why they are where they are. There is a strong desire to know whether or not we are doing whatever it is that we came to do.

Our purpose in life changes as we move through the learning that is taking place on a soul level. We are all here to learn, to wake up, and to remember that which we already know. In fact, we work hard at not remembering all that we know, just so we can learn the lessons we have created for ourselves in any one lifetime.

When we are born, and before our educational system begins to educate us in the ways of rational, analytical thinking, we know who we are and why we are here. By the time we reach the end of the first grade, we have begun to forget our primary purpose and have taken on the role of student of the left brain hemisphere and its thinking. Originally, the left brain was simply a filter, a tool for helping the right hemisphere put out what it was receiving. Through years of inaccurate thinking and pressure, the left brain began to take on a dominant role, and to speak for the ego, as though it were the wisdom within.

It is little wonder that the question of career and job changes comes up as frequently as it does. Before anyone asks the question of whether or not to change jobs, they should see why they are asking the question in the first place. If your mind gives you a question, or begins to have you ponder a situation, you can be certain that the answer is already right before you, and in all probability the answer is yes. If the energy that you are feeling is content with everything else that is going on in your life, the question of change would not arise in the first place.

Regardless of how some people may try to disguise it, they are not happy and they are unable to realize this fact because they are locked into a thought system which limits their perspective and aspirations. Know that your soul is constantly urging you, very quietly, to wake up, to know who you are and to be in harmony with its inner urging.

QUESTIONS

Q: I feel as though I am either stuck, or constantly swimming upstream.

Sometimes I think I should go in a different direction, but I don't know where to go and I've put so much work into being where I am. What should I do?

A: When we are in harmony with our inner voice and the natural flow of the Universe, doors open easily for us. When a door closes, the Universe is telling us to look in another direction, that our energy is not harmonious with this particular path. When we find we are swimming upstream, we are going against the natural flow. We can make life difficult or we can make it easy. It's our choice. It doesn't have to be difficult in order for us to learn and to be able to help others.

Q: I am presently in medical school, working very hard. Sometimes I wonder if I should have to spend so much of my lifetime giving up my private life and moments in order to be a healer. Couldn't this be easier?

A: Zen masters have taught us that we have to put forth the energy in order to have happen that which we wish to take place. There is a difference between swimming upstream, going against the flow, and working hard to achieve a goal. One lifetime is but a blink of an eye in the total picture of our developing soul. You have probably spent many lifetimes learning the art of healing in one way or another and now you are working to remember it. Don't discount the academic information you are acquiring now. After all, at some point it came from someone's intuition.

Q: Does it matter what I do for a career? Isn't it true that we all get to the same place anyway? I could work or not work and still get there.

A: It is true that ultimately we all get to the same point. However, in life it is the journey, not the destination that counts. You can make the journey an interesting one or one that is boring. As you make your journey interesting, you create learning situations for yourself that help your soul to grow and to be nourished. It doesn't matter how you make the journey, but it would be nice if you took time to smell the roses along the way.

Q: What is my purpose of being here this time around?

A: So many of us think that we have to have a lofty purpose—to save the world, not realizing that saving the world begins within. We are so busy looking outside of ourselves for that purpose, we fail to learn who we really are until it is too late. It is important to work on changing the self, not the world. Imposing your own answers on the world is not allowing others to follow their own goals, to march to their own drummer. No matter how insignificant you may think your role on this planet is, know that you would be sorely missed if you were not here. No other soul can fill your space. It is not the job you are doing, but the energy you bring to the planet.

Q: I feel as though I should make a move to another city in order to further my career, but I seem to block when it comes to knowing exactly where to go.

A: The Universe gives us signs and guideposts that tell us we are on the right path and going in the right direction. For example, I had known for three years that I was going to be moving from Norfolk, Virginia, but I didn't know where. After facilitating a workshop in Pennsylvania one of the participants approached me and said that she had a feeling I was going to move to Boston.

What followed was a series of "signs," e.g., the few times I turned on the T.V., either the Boston Celtics were playing or it was the Public

Broadcasting System flashing BOSTON across the screen. On more than one occasion, I would be flying across country and discover that I was sitting next to someone from Boston on the airplane. Just when I was beginning to feel that I was making all of this up, I looked up (I was driving around Virginia) and I was following a car that had a Boston University sticker on it.

These are important signs in life and it is important to notice them. The Universe gives us tangible signs for a reason, which is what our left brain likes, to show us that we are on the right path. If you are unclear about what to do, ask for a sign.

Once I made my move to New England, other positive affirmations followed. I began to book more seminars and workshops, and opportunities opened up at a hospital for working with staff and patients. I was also able to continue my research (exploring the connection between intuitive medical information and traditional medical information in an effort to bring the two together in a constructive manner) with a medical professor at Brown University.

Q: How can I trust what I am feeling?
A: Start by discerning "what" you are feeling or sensing. Then act on the information that you receive (as long as it's reasonable.) Finally, watch for feedback.

Q: How will I know when to quit?
A: When things are so difficult that it is virtually impossible to accomplish anything, and you feel that you take two steps backward for each step you take forward, look in another direction. Life does not have to be difficult. Making it less so may be as easy as letting go of a difficult or impossible goal. Who set the goal in the first place? Was it your original goal or that of your parents or someone else in authority?

Perhaps it was a goal you set because of shoulds and oughts. Letting go will free you to move to a higher purpose which may presently be masked by excessive energy in the wrong direction. Just remember when you are on the right path, things aren't as difficult. The exception to this rule is the person who makes it to where he wants to be in spite of hard times. Consider, it may not have had to be via "hard times." Could it be she (or he) created the hard times because her belief system said only through hard work do we reach our goals?

Q: How do I know I have made the right choice?

A: It will feel right when you align the mental picture or thought of what you have decided upon with the feeling you get from your heart. Put yourself in a meditative state and relax. Ask your highest source of information for guidance and state verbally or mentally what you have decided to do. Then wait and see how it feels within your body. The correct answer will balance with the heart chakra. You will feel a warmth and centeredness there and know yours was the correct choice. If, on the other hand, you feel nervous or anxious then substitute your choice with other alternative choices. See which one feels the most comfortable.

Q: Do the right choices always reap rewards?

A: First, we have to ask ourselves if there is a wrong choice? Even what may seem to be wrong, could ultimately be the perfect choice for our soul at this point in time. Is it possible to be on the wrong path? We can evaluate our choices by our contentment with ourselves and make a choice because it is what *we* want to do and not something others expect of us.

Q: There is a job I would like to have, but someone else is in the position. I don't want to do anything harmful to them, yet I can't see anything else I would rather do.

A: One of the major problems with creating our life and career is to think that there is only one of anything. We forget that it is an abundant Universe and there is plenty for all . . . even jobs. You can visualize your ideal job, complete with salary and working conditions, release that vision and know that it, or something better, will manifest in your life. By visualizing what you wish to create in your life, you don't take away from someone else. Their soul/spirit is constantly manifesting for them as well. It is possible that the person in the job you want will be promoted or take a higher paying job elsewhere. As long as you visualize for the good of all you don't need to be worried. You do not have the power to manipulate another's soul, just your perception and creation of reality.

Q: I don't know what I want. Where do I start?

A: There are many individuals in this world who do not know what they want. Whenever I get a clear picture of what I want, it is there, almost immediately.

However, getting to this clarity may mean weeks or months of unconscious processing as to what it is I want.

One way to start to see what you want is to relax and visualize what you see yourself doing five, ten years from now. Look at or feel the picture in great detail, who is with you, where are you, what are you doing as a career, are you happy? If you are not happy, then look to see how you would change the picture and make that change in your mind. Be sure to put yourself in the picture.

After you have this image of yourself in the future, sit down with a pencil and paper and write out short-term goals (the next year), mid-term goals (the next five years) and long-term goals (the next ten years).

Be sure to make your goals reasonable and obtainable. For instance, don't have your goal be to lose one hundred pounds in one month. This is not only not realistic; it is not healthy.

If, for some reason, you don't obtain one of your goals, don't judge yourself as having failed. Simply know that your goal has changed and you are not putting the energy into it that you were initially.

Goals, like everything else in life, need to be flexible and able to flow with the Universal energy.

Q: I don't feel that I am free to run my own life. I have too many demands made on me that I have to meet.

A: No matter how you frame the question, you are always responsible for your own life and for the demands made upon you. If you feel others take advantage of you then you are allowing them to do so.

Remember, you create your own reality and you attract to you as you think. If you don't feel that you are a free spirit and able to control your life, start asking for help from your highest source of information and know that it will come.

MEDITATION

Asking life questions is probably one of the most difficult areas to focus on and to see clearly. It is important to take a sufficient amount of time, thirty minutes or so, to relax before you begin to ask your source for information about you and your future

After you are relaxed, ask yourself the following questions:

Am I happy? What does it mean to be happy?

If not, what is keeping me from being happy? What am I looking for?

What about my life/career do I like?

When I look back on my life from the age of 100, what will I like about it?

When I look back on my life from the age of 100, what would I like to change?

Thank your higher self for this information. Request that you be given "guideposts" that you are going in the right direction, and then watch for them!

The fact that the mind rules the body is, in spite of its neglect by biology and medicine, the most fundamental fact which we know about the process of life.

—Franz Alexander, M.D.

We must remove the word "impossible" from our vocabulary. As David Ben-Gurion once observed in another context, "Anyone who doesn't 't believe in miracles is not a realist." Moreover, when we see how terms like "spontaneous remission" or "miracle" mislead and confuse us, then we will learn. Such terms imply that the patient must be lucky to be cured. It could be that healing takes place when we let go of trying to force wellness.

They are not acts of God. Remember that one generation's miracle may be another*s scientific fact. Do not close your eyes to acts or events that are not always measurable. They happen by means of an inner energy available to all of us. That's why I prefer term like "creative" or "self-induced" healing, which emphasize the patient's active role.

—Bernie S. Siegel, M.D.
Love, Medicine and Miracles

CHAPTER FOUR

Health

Robbie Gass once put out a flyer that began, "You will receive a body. You may like it or hate it, but it will be yours for the entire period this time around." All too often the concept of taking care of the body is forgotten, put on hold for another day, or ignored completely with the hope that the body will take care of itself. It does—perhaps not the way we would like for it to take care of itself—but it does form itself according to our thoughts and thinking patterns.

Of all of the realities that your belief system creates, your physical well-being is perhaps the most important. If you are not healthy in body, how can you begin to believe that you can create abundance and happiness in your life? Western society's belief in physicians is overwhelming. The belief systems between patient and doctor affect not only the ultimate recovery of the patient, but the belief in the ability of one's body to heal itself.

It has been my experience in working with physicians, as we apply non-traditional intuitive approaches to medicine, that it is about five years after graduating from medical school that they begin to realize they don't have all of the answers. Patients that should get better die, and patients that don't have a chance of living live. What happens? Are these miracles? Or just tomorrow's science made known today? It is my feeling that in ten years the work we are researching with the mind/body relationship will be common knowledge, the way things work naturally.

The first step on the road to a healthy body is the awareness that your thoughts are creating your physical body. Worries that you carry around with you express themselves in wrinkles and frown lines, burdens or weights show up as backaches, and people or problems you can't stomach become ulcers, gastritis, colitis.

The body is a wonderful barometer not only of what is going on within your own mind, but around you in your environment. It will quickly inform you it needs rest, food (carbohydrates or protein) or exercise. You intuitively know if you have received too much sun, or if you should consult a physician about some problem that is worrying you.

Instantly, when you are injured, you know if you have broken a bone, or if it is just a superficial injury, such as a sprain. Because you know these things doesn't mean that you pay attention to them. In this country we think if we aren't active then we aren't being productive, and being productive may mean continuing to work even when we don't feel like it.

If we push our bodies to the limit, e.g., working long hours when our intuition tells us to rest, drinking coffee to keep going, we are sending the body a message that it will have to yell loudly in order for us to pay attention. Loudly may be too late. It could mean hospitalization or some other serious illness.

That said, the pain you feel may not belong to you. As you open up spiritually you become sensitive to the pain of others. In effect, you become a sponge and soak up all information, pain, and feelings around you. The next time you experience a headache ask yourself, "What's the matter with my head?" If it's your headache, your head will hurt more, if it isn't your headache, if it belongs to someone else, it will go away.

QUESTIONS

Q: If meditation is as important as people say it is, then why do I have to exercise or eat properly? It seems I should be able to do whatever I want, meditate, and be healthy.

A: We are here in human form and it is important to take care of the form. The form we chose was created to move. The body was meant to be in motion, to be enjoyed. Meditation can do many things and there certainly are examples of yogis who only meditated and lived to ripe old ages. However, you are living in the stress-induced

environment of the modern world, and unless you are a yogi, you
need to eat a healthy diet and exercise along with your relaxation/
meditation time.

Q: You mention eat properly. Doesn't what I "eat" buy into my
belief system? If I think it is good for me then it is, and if I think it is
bad then it will do harm?

A: Basically yes. The problem is that we have all been educated
that the only way to be healthy is to eat three well-balanced meals
a day. We are slowly changing our beliefs to read, "It is better to eat
several small meals," "we don't need three meals a day," and "red
meat is not necessarily good for you." The fitness craze sweeping the
country has substituted one belief system for another, all concerned
with what we put into our mouths. Technically you might be
able to eat anything you desired with no ill effect—it all turns to
carbohydrate to be burned in the end—but mentally it would be
difficult for you to break away from years of programming about
nutrition.

Q: Is there a natural way to slow down the aging process?

A: Individuals I know that seem to have "slowed" the aging
process never think about how old they are. In fact, if asked, they
may have to do a bit of calculation; it just isn't something that
concerns them. Getting older is a fact of life, but it doesn't mean that
our bodies have to fall apart on us or that we have to look our age.

Q: I am afraid that if I get in touch with my higher self I will
know when I am going to die, and that scares me.

A: We all know when we are going to die. It is only when death
rides on our left shoulder that we can begin to live. It is good to be
aware of when you are "scripting" your death because you may
want to change it. We usually "script" our death according to the
death of the parent of our same sex. They are our role model and
their illnesses and death are the only model we have for getting out
of this reality. Look to see what age you think you are going to die.
As you get older you may discover that you have chosen an age that
is actually quite young and you can change it.

Through the research of Dr. Bruce Lipton and other leading-edge scientists, new discoveries have been made about the interaction between your mind and body and the processes by which cells receive information. This research shows that genes and DNA do not control our biology, that instead DNA is controlled by signals from outside the cell, including the energetic messages emanating from our thoughts. Using simple language, illustrations, humor, and everyday examples, he demonstrates how the new science of *Epigenetics* is revolutionizing our understanding of the link between mind and matter and the profound effects it has on our personal lives and the collective life of our species.

MEDITATION

Relax in a favorite chair or place. Loosen your clothing and put your feet up. Notice if any part of your body is uncomfortable and adjust yourself so that it doesn't bother you. Try not to think of problems or solutions. Take a deep breath. As you inhale, visualize a warm white light flowing down from the top of your head, moving slowly through your body and out the soles of your feet. Imagine that everything that you need and desire is flowing to you as you breathe in.

As you exhale, draw the white light up the outside of your body until it reaches the top of your head and begins to circulate around and down. Exhale out all of the things that you don't feel are beneficial to you: poor health, jealousy, anxiety, poverty.

After you have done this for a few minutes, visualize your physical body. If you can't do this at first, then sense it, touching that portion of yourself which may ache or be experiencing pain or discomfort.

Next, direct the white light to that portion of your body you feel needs healing. Feel the warmth and intensity of the light as it moves in and through this area. Know that you and the Universal source of energy, of which you are a part, are healing your body, restoring it to perfection.

Another shift I see that really impresses me is a new respectability for intuition in corporate settings. Now people are willing to say, "I just feel this is going to work."

—John Naisbitt, *Megatrends*

CHAPTER FIVE

Business Decisions

The use of the "mind" is playing a more prominent role in business management and decisions today than ever before. Some feel that in fifteen years using intuition to make business decisions will be perfectly normal, as right-brain thinking gains more prestige due to competitive demands placed on this country from markets such as Japan, where intuition in the workplace has brought considerable profit, and by American blue-chip companies' acceptance of the approach. Among the forerunners in this mental revolution are companies such as Arco, Dow Corning, IBM, Kodak, etc.

What is happening because of the mental revolution is that more and more executives at the top are realizing that making decisions is not a function exclusively of the analytical left-brain, it is an integration of both the left and the intuitive right. Simply stated, right brain management is allowing the intuitive, creative side of the brain to have a voice in making decisions in tandem with the analytical left side.

In the corporate world this theory is referred to as whole brain thinking.

The word used is "hunch" and it has been used by many decision-making executives who frequently make decisions against the statistics in front of them, preferring to rely on that "gut" feeling, and many times to their benefit. The history of business is replete with data suggesting that some who totally relied on available information and research made the wrong decisions based on those findings. One recent example was Coca-Cola's decision to market a new formula for "Coke."

Of course, doing "homework" continues to be necessary before making financial or business decisions. However, information, which is assessed by the left-brain, tends to be more profitable when integrated with input from the right brain.

As whole brain thinking gains respectability, more big corporations are exposing their CEOs to seminars on the subject and are finding the results beneficial in marketing, selecting personnel, predicting future trends, and purchasing equipment.

Since whole brain thinking is a new-age concept, many feel awkward when asking for help and frequently preface their questions concerning right brain thinking with, "I know this is a dumb question, but . . . ," because they feel they should already have the analytical or business acumen to know the answer.

QUESTIONS

Below is a sampling of some of the more general questions asked at whole brain seminars:

Q: How will I know when it's the right time to buy property?

A: Owning property starts with a seed planted in the subconscious, which, if nurtured, will grow until it matures into a full feeling that you want to own something that is part of the earth. Just as we put out thoughts that draw certain people to us, so it is with home ownership. Perhaps it will begin by turning into a wrong street, only to find the home of your dreams with a "For Sale" sign on the lawn.

Q: How do I tell when it's the "right" time to begin a business venture?

A: If it feels right, go for it. But, if on the other hand, you feel nervous, anxious or unsure and experience a certain tightness in your head when you think about it, it is best to postpone your decisions until these uneasy feelings leave.

Begin by assessing your emotions, center on yourself by relaxing and moving inward. The morning hours may be best for this exercise, for your activity is at its lowest point and your mind shouldn't be crowded with the activities of the day.

One final note, and this is to those who may wish to speculate more liberally. It is possible to control certain fundamentals of our environment, which means it is possible to be a wild card winner. A case in point is Ray Kroc who purchased the McDonald hamburger chain, going against the advice of his lawyer and financial advisor.

The payoff: The Golden Arches!

EXERCISE

For problem solving:

Pull all available data together and review as you would for any type of decision. Put the data aside and go for a walk, take a nap, or have a cup of coffee. Wait for the insight to "pop" into your mind.

Prior to going to sleep put the "problem" in the hands of your higher self and ask that you be given a dream with the information you need. Write down your dream upon awakening.

Relax in a sitting or reclining state. Place the problem before you in your mind and ask yourself for a solution. When you sense a picture, word, or thought or other type of information see how it feels on your body. Look to your heart chakra . . . is there a centeredness there? A feeling of well-being when you get the answer? Or, are you anxious, unclear? If the latter is the case, take the question back to your higher self and keep looking for the solution that feels most comfortable on your physical body and your heart chakra.

VISUALIZATION

Before an important meeting:

Relax, allow white light to flow throughout your body, starting with your head and working its way down to your feet. Imagine that you are in the meeting room with the person or persons you will be with. See everyone, including yourself, in great clarity. Have the situation take place exactly as you would like to see it, include a feeling of warmth, love, and friendliness as you do this. Surround this picture with a pink balloon, release it, and know that this, or something better, will manifest for you.

When love beckons to you, follow him, though his ways are hard and steep.

And when his wings enfold you, yield to him, though the sword hidden among his pinions may wound you.

And when he speaks to you, believe in him, though his voice may shatter your dreams as the north winds lays waste the garden.

For even as love crowns you so shall he crucify you. Even as he is for your growth so he is for your pruning.

Even as he ascends to your height and caresses your tenderest branches that quiver in the sun,

So shall he descend to your roots and shake them in their clinging to the earth.

Like sheaves of corn he gathers you unto himself.

He threshes you to make you naked.

He shifts you to free you from your husks. He grinds you to whiteness.

He kneads you until you are pliant,

And then he assigns you to his sacred fire, that you may become sacred bread for God's sacred feast.

All these things shall love do unto you that you may know the secrets of your heart, and in that knowledge become a fragment of Life's heart.

—Kahlil Gibran, *The Prophet*

CHAPTER SIX

Relationships

Relationships may be our most difficult lesson in any one lifetime. Regrettably, few people listen to the resonance from within themselves that can help them find not only where they belong, but with whom they belong.

If you are someone who can't stand the idea of being alone, I suggest that you learn to *enjoy* being alone with yourself. Find out who you are, treat yourself with special care, in short, use the time to learn to love yourself. Then consider the question, why do you want to be in a relationship? What will you bring to the union?

At the same time, if you truly desire a relationship, it will show up. Gently affirm to yourself that they are coming. You would not have the desire for partnership if it were not attached to something.

For months, prior to leaving my life in Virginia, I repeated affirmations that I would meet the perfect partner, or compliment, for me. I was going strictly on trust in the Universe. I didn't have a steady income, and yet, I had signed a lease on an apartment in Providence (for considerably more than I was making in my newly formed training and consulting business.) In fact, almost all of my business contacts were still in Virginia.

Everything fell into place. The apartment I found was in the process of being renovated (it was gutted when I saw it), and the landlady kindly agreed to let me select the paint colors. She allowed pets (I had two dogs), and there was easy access to the first floor so that I could move in my grand piano. There was even an extra bedroom that I didn't know about until the day I moved in. This extra room turned out to be symbolic of making "space" for someone else.

My year in Providence was a year of discovering my inner self. I constantly asked myself if I had made the right decision to leave. During this time, I used my dream teller to help me find answers. For example, on one occasion I asked, "What's going on in my life?" (Although this is a very general question, I believe our heart knows the real question and answers.) In my dream there was an airplane sitting on the runway, waiting to take off. But boarding I said, "I have to go to my exercise studio." When I got to the studio a "Closed" sign was across the door, so I returned to the airport, walked by Katherine Ross (star of *The Graduate)* and boarded the plane.

Not only did I graduate from that life, I married a Robinson, lived in Scarborough, Maine (our witnesses at our Glastonbury, England wedding were from Scarborough, England) and I grow parsley, sage, rosemary and thyme in my garden. Was my intuition telling me all of that in just one dream, or was I creating my future in the dream? Does it make any difference? At the least, the dream told me that there was nothing I could work out. It was time to go.

After I moved to R.I. there were many nights when I could not sleep because I was conflicted about dissolving my sixteen-year marriage. Had I made a mistake? This was my "security" drama . . . leaving a new home, an "important career," and lots of security. Frequently I would fall asleep asking my *dream teller* for guidance. Early one morning, I had one of the last dreams in my "leaving" series. I was riding in a car with my ex-husband when the road we were on dead-ended. We got out of the car and walked through a graveyard. I ended up in a house that was sinking into the mud. The backside of the house was totally open—it had no walls. When I walked out of the house I looked down and saw that I was carrying a bag of garbage in each hand. I put the bags down and continued on.

There was one more dream in which my husband and I shook hands. This phase of my life was complete and I was ready to move forward. The next night my *dream teller* began to prepare me for marriage. I dreamed of a loveseat, I purchased a wedding gown, chose my bridesmaids and picked flowers—all of which was symbolic. I did not wear a wedding gown or have bridesmaids at our wedding.

In the first edition of *Intuitions,* I wrote about soul mates and twin souls. Now, I am not as sure about these concepts as I was then. I have no doubt that there are very special souls with whom we connect, but as with the dolphins, putting our words and concepts on these energies may limit them. Never in my wildest imagination could I have known what Michael would be like. He was far, far different from anyone I had ever known, let alone dated.

Three days after I moved to R.I., I canceled a program in Chicago in order to fill in for another trainer at the Monroe Institute. It didn't make sense for me to do this, but I did. Because I was emotionally drained from the move, the most I could do was coordinate the technical aspects of the program while my co-trainer handled all of the *spiritual emergencies.* Midweek, I realized that there was one participant I didn't know at all. This is highly unusual, because I was facilitating a seven-day residential setting with only 24 participants. That evening I sat next to him at dinner (it was also the only vacant seat.) His name was Michael.

"I find it very intimidating that you can read my mind," he said.

"I know, why is that?" as I wondered, why do I have this intense feeling in my heart when he asks that question? Do I intimidate all men? Does this mean I'll never find my partner?

Before he could respond to my answer, my co-trainer pulled me away from the table.

As everyone was preparing to depart the last day, I felt a tap on my shoulder. It was the same man. "I understand that you do readings. I don't know what they are, but would you do one for me? I would like you to help me figure out a dream I had the other night."

After he described the woman in his dream I knew that she was a very special soul mate, soon to enter his life.

"What can you tell me about my soul mate in this life?" he asked.

"You've touched her hand. I also see the letter M. (I later pondered if the M was for me? An upside down W? Or, was I just wrong on this account?)

"It's Winter," Michael thought but didn't say anything. He did start to think of every woman whose hand he had touched. He later said that whenever he thought about what I had said, he would think that it was me.

During the following summer, I was writing *Intuitions* and deadlines seemed to be the only thing on my mind. I was also paying strict attention to my dream life in order to process how dreams worked for me. One of my discoveries in living alone was that my dogs got up early and go out (5:00 a.m.). I got into the habit of letting them out and going back to bed. During these early morning hours of sleep, I would dream the answers to my dream questions, have lucid dreams or out-of-body experiences. One morning I was in an out-of-body state with a friend I was sure was "The" man in my future. We were engrossed in trying to pull a woman out of her body. (I should have known then that this man was involved with someone else.) A stranger suddenly appeared in the dream, and kissed me.

"How dare you come into my dream and kiss me!" Waves from a deep green ocean rolled over me, *"and, you are hypnotizing me!)* I woke up.

A few months later, re-reading my dream journal, I saw that I had written *I like the kiss of this tall, blonde, alien man.*

I not only write down dreams, I write down words and sentences that I hear in the night. On December 22, 1987, I wrote: exhibits, talking with others, and waiting for Michael.

QUESTIONS

Q: Will I automatically recognize the love of my life?

A: When I was younger, and less experienced, I would have answered, "Of course you will." But the real answer is, "Not necessarily. We don't always recognize our future." The Universe has ways of bringing humility to us. My *anam`cara* (soul friend) was staring me in the face and I couldn't see him, as this example illustrates:

During a workshop in Boston, a participant (Stan) came up to me and said, "I'm attending your workshop because my roommate said that it would be great!"

"Who is your roommate?"

"Michael Robinson."

"I don't know a Michael Robinson."

"You met him at the Monroe Institute last spring. He lives in Maine."

These are the situations I hate to get myself into, because here is someone who clearly knows who I am—so much so he sends his roommate to my workshop. I should know who he is; after all, I spent seven days as his facilitator in an intensive program. I just couldn't remember, or bring up a psychic picture of this man.

A few weeks after the workshop, I received a call from Stan setting up a private session for Michael. "Just drop him a card and tell him when and where to show up."

Two weeks later, when Michael walked in the door, I recognized him. "He's very cute," I thought.

I didn't realize that this man was someone with whom I was spending eternity. I loved his energy, so much that I talked about it . . . a lot. After the session, as Michael prepared to leave, he invited me to visit him in Maine that weekend. I took him up on his offer.

A few weeks after my weekend in Maine, I was with my friend Swami, in Boynton Canyon, Arizona when two ravens landed four feet in front of me. From the comer of my eye, I saw Swami giving me one of her *knowing* looks.

"Partnership is at hand," she said.

Later that evening, as we sat around a table in the small cabin we had rented, Swami pulled out her Mother Peace Tarot deck. "I have a layout that works for relationship. I have been using it for several weeks and it works every time."

"There is no one in my life right now, Swami.

"Come on. Just give me a name."

"Read my lips—no one I can do a layout with." How, I wonder, do you tactfully tell a Swami to "bug off?"

"Come on, Winter. It's just for fun, and it works. Use anybody."

Finally, after what seemed an hour of saying, "No," I gave in, "Oh, all right, use Michael."

"Who's Michael?"

"Just a friend. That's all. We went skiing together recently."

Swami began the layout. "He doesn't know what to do. This is a major, major transformational relationship."

To be honest, I don't think I was listening to all she was saying.

I noticed her hand shaking and, for once and possibly the first time in her life, Swami seemed to have difficulty speaking.

"You're going to marry this man."

"No, Swami. Not Michael, he's *just* a friend. We both know I'm probably very close to another relationship, and I think that you are probably picking up on that energy."

The last two days I was in Arizona, I was very sick. I felt as though something were trying to overtake me. All I could do was lie in bed and dream. The morning I was to leave, I had a lucid dream.

"I want to be with my soul friend." Immediately, I was making love with a man with a marvelous energy. It didn't last long, because a girlfriend who was with me woke me up. I wasn't happy to have this wonderful dream experience end in this manner.

"Why did you do that?"

"I thought you were having a nightmare."

At the time I was unaware in that I had filled my entire life with work and female friends. There was no space for a man to be in my life, even though I said I wanted a relationship. Well, that's not quite true. I had a room in my apartment that was virtually empty. It was as though this room were waiting for *him*.

The first thing I did when I returned to Rhode Island was to place a call to Michael. Listening to his telephone ring, I thought,

"I hope Stan doesn't answer. I really want to talk to Michael and yet I have no good excuse." (Why do we need an excuse to talk to someone other than the fact that we want to?)

Michael answered.

We decided that Michael would come down to Providence the coming weekend. We wanted to discuss the work of Carlos Castaneda.

In the meantime, I was questioning, "Where would a man fit into my life?" I realized that I didn't need a man to make me happy or fulfilled. I was happy and I felt fulfilled as a human and as a woman.

The day we were to talk of Castaneda, we did everything but! We went to Newport and walked the cliffs, looked at boats, and talked of magic and other unknowns of the Universe. At one point we walked out onto a rocky shoreline to see the waves and ocean more clearly, and I took his arm. As this long, fun-filled day came to a close, we finally settled in to talk about Castaneda. It was chilly, so I pulled out an old Hudson's Bay blanket and threw it over the two of us as we sat and chatted in front of a fire.

It felt so comfortable, and so normal. As we talked, (he was so close to me I could see the almost invisible, feathery tips of his eyelashes and the thin lines under his eyes that crinkled when he smiled) I realized that I was looking at him through something sheer, slightly transparent—a veil. The veil slowly lifted and I recognized Michael for the first time.

One of my inner selves, most likely the "I am a proper, Southern woman," became loud and clear, "What do I do with this? Here I am with this cute, very eligible bachelor who probably has numerous women chasing after him. Do I tell him about this veil, about the dreams and out-of-body experiences with him? What is he thinking right now? What do I say? What am I going to do with this awareness?

The reality of the situation was that I threw the blanket off, stood up and announced, "I'm going to brush my teeth and go to bed."

I heard the front door open as Michael went out to the car to bring in his sleeping bag. Once back inside, he tossed it on the futon in the guest room, turned and smiled at me. Teeth brushed, I came out of the bathroom. And then, did I step forward? Did he?

Michael put his arms around me, gently kissed me good night, and asked, "What are you thinking?"

"What are you thinking?"

"I asked you first."

Could I be honest and still maintain a friendship with this person I was coming to like so much? Could I tell only a partial truth and live with myself? What did I have to lose? If I was honest and it scared him, I would blow a wonderful friendship with someone with whom I was very comfortable. On the other hand, if I didn't tell the complete truth, we might remain as friends when there was potential for so much more. Was what I was feeling real? Was it just sexual energy?

I told him that I didn't want him to spend the night in the guest room.

When Michael took me in his arms, I fit. It was as though we were made from a single mold, the two halves linking so perfectly.

Back to the question about recognizing our future partner. I think Michael had more of a clue in thinking, *it's Winter,* than I did. In hindsight I see that I received many messages about my future partner, but I was also very selective and edited the information coming in. For instance, I had several dreams in which I was with a stranger who was tall and blonde. Because this description did not "fit" what I expected my future partner to look like, I ignored these dreams. Also, in looking back over my journals, I came across an old tarot reading that a friend had done for me. "I see the beginning of romance. This man will be blonde; will live in the country, loves nature and home. He is well liked, honorable and sound in judgment.""

Perhaps, as Michael Talbot *(Holographic Universe)* would have said, there are several holograms that tell us of our future. Ultimately, I chose the one with the strongest energy, and the one I had been creating with Michael prior to reincarnating.

QUESTIONS

Q: I'm certain that I have met my *anam cara,* or soul mate, and I'm married. What should I do?

A: I can't think of any time when I would advise an individual to leave a relationship, certainly not for someone else. It is important to know who you are and what you want before leaping into a relationship with another individual. If you aren't happy with yourself no one else will be able to make you happy, and you will find yourself on the fast road to disaster. Not only that, you will recreate the same relationship again and again, because it is you doing the creating.

Listen to your inner voice speak to you about how you feel. Are you happy with your life? It is not your present partner who makes you miserable, only you can claim responsibility for how you feel. If you aren't happy, why aren't you happy? What are the things that you used to like to do that you no longer have time for? What is keeping you from doing them? Are these things fulfilling, or are they part of an endless search? Are they a way of keeping busy? Remember, we all change constantly. We are not the same person we were in the grocery store this morning, let alone the same person we were last year.

I did not leave my ex-husband for anyone other than myself. I wasn't happy. I didn't have the energy that I knew was once inside me. John didn't take the energy from me. I let it burn out by allowing myself to assume a role that wasn't true to my spirit. It eventually caught up with me. Could I have remained in my first marriage and worked things out? I don't think so. The fact is I was returning to my true self—a self that I had ignored for many years. I was not the same person my husband married. If I were to live, I had to leave.

Q: How do I know when a relationship is right for me?

A: Listen to your inner voice. How do you feel when you are with this person? Is it all sexual attraction or is there more? Is there an attraction you can't quite label? Are you your true self when with this person? Know that if the only qualities you are attracted to in this individual are based on some type of emotional or financial insecurity within yourself the relationship is in trouble from the very beginning. It is easy to let our logical brain tell us this is the perfect relationship because of the material things it offers, but we must be willing to look at our "gut" feelings when evaluating the total picture.

Q: Does everyone have a soulmate or twin soul?

A: These days I prefer to use the Celtic term *anam cara*, our soul friend.

With our *anam cara* we share our innermost self, our mind, and our heart. They are our teacher, companion, and best friend. In this love, we are accepted for who we are; there is no mask or pretension. We are understood and we feel at home.

In *Annam Cara*, John O'Donohue writes of the depth of awareness and reverence for presence with another. "Awareness is one of the greatest gifts you can bring to your friendship. Many people have an anam cara of whom they are not truly aware. This lack of awareness cloaks the friend's presence and causes feelings of distance and absence. Sadly, it is often loss that awakens presence, by then it is too late. It is wise to pray for a grace of recognition. Inspired by awareness, you may then discover beside you the anam cara of whom your longing has always dreamed."

Q: Does this mean that the relationship is perfect?

A: That's exactly what it means. But perfect doesn't mean that you aren't working through the problems of your shadow, the compliment of what you show to the world. It may be difficult, but extremely satisfying as you clear away the garbage you have created throughout many lifetimes.

Q: Is it possible that we won't meet our anam cara?
A: It is possible that we won't recognize them.
Q: What about soulmates?
A: It is my belief that soul mates are souls we have been with through many lifetimes, ones we have married frequently, and ones who have been our business partners, ones with whom we have both created and worked through karma.

Q: You say this as though we have many soulmates.
A: I think so. That's why there are any number of individuals we can fall in love with and be happy with, at least until we have worked through the reason of our being together.

Q: Why do people fall "out of love?"
A: It's not falling out of love, it's finishing our roles together. Relationships, like everything else, move to a rhythm, a cycle. Once we are in touch with this rhythm, we know when it is time to follow the energy to the next stage in our life.

Q: Are you saying that separation and divorce shouldn't be seen as such a traumatic and negative thing?
A: Exactly. I ended a long-term relationship. We had come together during college and supported each other both financially and emotionally. That was our role for that point in time. As we changed, our needs and concepts of what relationships should be changed. I realized that my husband was really my brother and that was the type of love I felt for him. I don't love him any less after this realization, but I recognized he wasn't the person who could help me grow the most. I wasn't the one to help him grow.

Q: What brought you to this realization?
A: There was something missing in my life, something I could not name, but something I had been looking for all of my life.

Q: What do you think it was?

A: Myself.

Q: Why do some people settle for less in a relationship?

A: They don't know how to "trust" that the Universe always provides and that everything is on schedule. We have to learn to trust and to be patient. Many individuals start counting their chronological age, "I'm 34, if I don't marry now I never will, or I'll never have a family," etc.

Q: Do you think people know that they are settling for less?

A: Oh, yes. Many friends, now divorced, have said that on their wedding day they knew it wouldn't last. At the same time that first marriage, or relationship, made them who they are today.

Q: What advice would you give to someone waiting for his or her life's partner?

A: First, don't sit around "waiting for your partner." That suggests that, in some way, you expect this person to meet and fulfill your "needs." This attitude isn't healthy.

EXERCISE *(for present relationship)*

Sit quietly, take a deep breath, close out the external and focus your thoughts inward. Relax and ask yourself, one question at a time:

How did you feel when you first met your current love?

Was it strictly a physical attraction or was there more to it?

Were you attracted to this person by some intangible magical aspect?

Did you feel you had known this person before?

How do you feel about him/her now?

How does he/she feel about you?

Do you still feel there is someone else *out there*?

Do you want to be with him/her for the rest of your life?

Could you spend days/weeks with him or her, without a physical relationship, and be content and happy?

Are the two of you seldom alone? Is it frequently necessary to be part of a crowd? Can you talk at a deep level about yourself, your desires, fears, etc, or do you edit what you say, fearing your partner won't understand, won't be interested?

How do you feel when together? Are you peaceful, contented or are you anxious to keep moving?

Do you think something is missing in this relationship?

The above list may be incomplete. You may have personal questions of a specific nature which may need to be addressed. These should be added to the list and answered honestly and as intuitively as possible. Go with the first answer that pops into your mind. Don't discount it or rationalize it away.

EXERCISE

Sit or lie in a relaxed position. Imagine the white light is coming down from the Universe and flowing through your head down to your feet, then circulating around to your head again. Let the white light continue to flow in this manner for a few minutes. Now ask that your higher self, or the highest source of information that you contact, be present. Affirm to this source and to the Universe that you are ready for your heart chakra to open. You are now ready to give and receive love.

In your mind's eye see the white light focusing on your heart area and then moving out into the Universe.

Affirm, "My perfect partner is coming to me.

I am love and I attract love to me. My partner is love and is attracted to me.

Use the term partner, soul mate, or companion, depending on what your intuition tells you to use. You will attract the one that is most perfect for you at this point in time.

Thank the Universe for its help and come back to the present, knowing that your perfect relationship is making its way to you.

Remember, when you have attracted that special someone to you, relationships are like roses . . . you must let them unfold, naturally.

It's the heart afraid of breaking that never learns to dance. It's the dream afraid of waking that never takes the chance. It's the one who won't be taken who cannot seem to give, and the soul afraid of dying that never learns to live.

CHAPTER SEVEN

Fear

Fear is a Universal emotion and can be ranked next to love and hate in intensity. It is possible that we do more things out of fear than from any other emotion that we experience.

Our society has raised us in a system of fear: fear of God, failure, success, measles, and terrorists, anyone different from ourselves. From early on religion taught us to fear that which we didn't know, in short, to fear the "I Am" part of ourselves. By being taught fear, and the fact that our lives are beyond our control, we have been limited in our understanding of how the Universe works. There is magic out there, and we create it every moment of our lives.

The key to conquering our fears is to become aware that the Universe is ordered and magical with a source of intelligence that helps us in times of need and/or trouble. Within this order is the fact that everything is on schedule, there are no accidents. What we give rise to as fear is just one more lesson that we have created in order to learn while we are here. Hopefully, we learn our lessons as they are presented in order not to have to repeat the same lesson lifetime after lifetime. All of life contains lessons, otherwise you wouldn't be here.

QUESTIONS

Q: Why am I so afraid to admit that I am psychic, or to get in touch with my psychic abilities?

A: Two reasons: you have been brought up in a society where our religious institutions teach us that the unknown is dark and evil, that you have no control over your life. No doubt you have been told, or have read somewhere, that psychic or metaphysical awareness is the work of the devil. The part of you that doesn't trust yourself believes some of this. The other part of this answer is that, perhaps, you have had a past life where you died for expressing what you believed in, for knowing there was more out there.

There is a part of you that doesn't want to repeat that experience.

I went through a similar experience when I was first developing my psychic awareness. I found I was afraid to admit I was psychic and would frequently do everything I could to block the experiences. One evening I had an out-of-body experience and past life regression (unplanned) simultaneously, where I became myself burning and dying as a witch. I knew I had red hair and green eyes, and I could see the faces of the onlookers as I burned. After that I thought, "So what's the worst thing that can happen to me for admitting that I am psychic? I die.

When we realize we come back again, and again, it isn't so frightening.

Q: Am I afraid of dying?

A: At some time in their lives, everyone is afraid of dying. They don't know what is out there, they think of missing those they love, and of all the things they thought they needed to accomplish. When we choose to move on to another reality, we can be assured that we have completed our purpose for this time around. If you're still here you have more work to do.

Individuals terminally ill usually move past their fears of death. They know there is more. Many report of seeing guardian angels by their beds and in their dreams. These angels are there to help make the journey easy. As the lyric from "The Rose" says,

"It's the soul afraid of dying that never learns to live."

Q: I have this deep-seated fear that no one likes me, thus, I spend a lot of my time doing things I don't really want to do in order to please others.

A: When you feel that others don't like you, it is a message to yourself that you don't like yourself. You attract to you as you think. If you don't like yourself, or are so intent on others liking or not liking you, then you will create that reflection of yourself in your environment. Learn to be good to yourself, to nourish yourself. Don't wait for a special occasion to wear perfume or dress up or to take a bubble bath. Do it now because you love yourself and want to be as good to yourself as you possibly can. As you come to love and appreciate yourself, the love within you can come forth and you will automatically draw to you those individuals who love you and love to be with you.

Q: I want to change my job, but I am afraid that I won't be able to find one that pays as well or that I will be happy doing.

A: Sit quietly and write out a list of qualities that you would like to have in a job. After you have put down everything that you can think of, take a moment to reflect on the list. Take a deep breath, close your eyes and imagine the white light, the creative force of the Universe coming down through the top of your head and flowing through your body. After you have the white light flowing strongly yet calmly throughout your body, visualize the future job exactly as you would like to have it, being sure to put yourself in the picture. Put it in a pink balloon and let go of it, affirming that it or something better will come to you. There is nothing more you need to do.

Q: I often feel my intuition telling me to do something, but I am afraid to follow it. What if it's wrong?

A: You'll never know if it's right or wrong unless you act on it. Our real intuition is always right. We may have to work and practice in order to sort out our chattering mind from our inner wisdom, which is our real source of knowledge. The only way to sort this out is to act on our intuitive hunches, to follow the feeling, the energy, where it leads us. The more we ignore it, either the weaker it will become, the more confused our lives will be, or the louder it will yell, but by then usually a rock has dropped on our head.

Q: I find I am letting my fears get the best of me. I am afraid to go out of the house, afraid to drive my car, afraid to see others, in short, afraid to live.

A: When your fears get the best of you, as yours have, it is time to seek professional counseling. You need to work with someone who will help you see clearly how you are letting irrational fears control your life. There are professionals who are familiar with past-life regression, relaxation therapy, and the laws of the Universe. This is the type of individual that you need to seek out in order to regain control of your life. There's nothing wrong in asking for help when we need it.

Q: It seems that I am hearing you say that if we trusted the Universe, the higher order of things, we would have no fears.

A: Fear is being out of touch with the master plan of the Universe, the Universal energy that flows through everyone. When we trust that it is there, guiding and protecting us, what more do we need?

Q: If there is this master plan, then why does it allow suffering and pain and the miseries of the world?

A: This is a universal question, one that as humans we may not completely understand. The miseries of the world that we see with our human eyes are a reflection of parts of our inner selves that need healing. They could be events that we have created in this lifetime to help us grow and to fully experience life. If we truly felt our connectivity with all of life, would we harm anyone or anything? In the same way, if there is no experience of loss or aloneness, how can we experience things like love, suffering? How can we have pain, which is a signal from our body that something is wrong? How would we know that we are healthy?

MEDITATION

Enter your relaxed state, watching your breathing and letting the white light flow through your body. Feel the white light extend outward from your heart into the Universe. Notice the warmth and energy that you feel when you do this. Ask your higher self to be with you and to protect you from any thought or feeling that is less than beneficial to you and your well-being.

Continue to feel relaxed, ask to be shown what you are afraid of. When you hear or see something that you fear, look at it in great detail. What is the worst possible scenario? When you think that you have a clear picture of the "worst that could happen," imagine, in any way that you can, that you are giving it to your higher self to take care of. Trust that you have released it.

During the day, whenever you feel your logical self creating fear(s), tell yourself, "I can create these fears if I like, but I'm going to give them to my higher self to take care of."

Sometimes it helps to make a list of our fears. Beside each fear write down how it is keeping you from living fully.

IF I HAD MY LIFE TO LIVE OVER

I'd like to make more mistakes next time.

I'd relax. I would limber up.

I would be sillier than I have been this trip.

I would take fewer things seriously. I would take more chances.

I would take more trips. I would climb more Mountains and swim more rivers.

I would eat more ice cream and less beans.

I would perhaps Have more actual troubles.

But I would have fewer imaginary ones.

You see, I'm one of those people who live Sensibly and Sanely, Hour after Hour, Day After Day.

Oh, I've had my moments, and if I had it to do over again, I'd have more of Them. In fact, I'd try to have nothing else.

Just moments, one after another, instead of living so many years ahead of each day.

I've been one of those persons who never goes anywhere without a thermometer, a hot Water bottle, a rain coat, and a parachute.

If I had to do it again, I would travel lighter than I have.

If I had my life to live over,

I would start barefoot earlier in the spring and stay that way Later in the fall. I would go to more dances; I would ride more merry-go-rounds.

I would pick more daisies.

—Nadine Satir, 85 years old, Louisville, KY

CHAPTER EIGHT

Listening

Remember that your intuition speaks softly, is patient, and will repeat the same message again and again until you get it.

Start listening to your heart, your intuition, by taking small steps, one at a time, in order to build your confidence in her ability to bring valuable guidance to you.

Be a risk-taker. Don't let yourself be motivated by inflexibility or a need for security.

Trust yourself. If you trust others more than you trust yourself, then you are programming your intuition to fail you.

Notice the affirmations that you give yourself on a daily basis. Do you say, "That problem is too difficult for me, I'll never find the answer?" Or, do you intuitively know that all answers are within you, and that if you ask a question, and let go of it, the answer will come? Make asking questions playful . . . a game.

"You have to ask a clear question and you ask one question at a time," Don Juan taught Carlos Castaneda. To ask more than one question at a time adds confusion to your answers, because you still get your answers, but they come all at once!

MEDITATION

Put yourself in your relaxed state and draw the white light in, down and through your body. Practice breathing deeply. Watch your breath flow in and out of your body as the white light flows through it. After you have done this for a while, ask that you make contact with your highest source of information, your guide, counselor, or whatever else you may wish to call it. When the counselor appears, ask whatever questions you desire.

Thank the counselor for the guidance you have received during this meditation.

TIPS FOR DISCOVERING YOUR INTUITION

Write down the last time you had an intuitive hunch and acted upon it.

Write down the last time you had an intuitive hunch and didn't act upon it. What happened?

How do you get your intuitive hunches?

Relax. Take a deep breath. Imagine that you are surrounded by a warm white light. Think of the things you like about your life, relationships, job.

Focus on the present moment. Try to solve a particular problem you are facing. Look to see who is with you and what you are doing to remedy the situation.

Put down all of the things that you know about the situation. Then put down what you would like to know about the situation. Follow the meditation exercise, which takes you to your guide in order to help you obtain the answers. Put down what you were told during the meditation, and see what additional questions come to mind.

Let go of the situation and be patient.

Another way to approach a problem would be to take a quiet moment to reflect on the situation. Then, using a pack of crayons, draw a picture that describes how you feel the issue.

Does the drawing give you insight? Look to see what colors you used, where you colored intensely, where you colored lightly, and where you didn't color at all.

Ask a friend what they see in your picture. Don't tell them what the picture is about. Let them "intuit" the information.

Finally, draw the picture as you would like to have the situation resolved. Don't forget to put yourself in the picture and use the color pink to surround the entire image. Shakti Gawain says that pink is the color of the heart and to use it brings harmony to that which we are creating.

Move on, knowing the answer will reveal itself.

Several times during the day say to yourself, "Tonight I will remember a dream that will bring me information about (this situation, problem, etc.). Then, before retiring, relax and say to yourself, "I will dream and I will remember the dream which will give me information about this situation.

Take a walk. Guess who the next person that you meet on the street will be. Male/female, old/young, what they will have on, etc.

Guess the amount of your next grocery bill without mentally trying to do the calculations in your head. Guess the amount of gas your car will need when you fill the tank.

Pretend that you are someone else, an inner being that lives inside of you. Have a friend ask you questions about your life, future, health, someone else's life and future.

Sit with a friend. Close your eyes and mentally ask to be in harmony with that individual. When you have been sitting for three minutes, take turns saying to each other the thoughts or images that have been coming to mind.

Express how you feel, or if you have any physical discomfort.

Center (relax) yourself. Go outside and find a tree.

Mentally ask the tree questions from the four directions:

North: What does the tree tell you?

East: How does it feel being a tree?

South: How do you feel?

West: What do you sense?

How do the answers resonate with what is on your heart?

With two other individuals take turns choosing a season or time of day, and think about it. Give no physical signs of what you have picked. Ask others in the group what they have picked up. In the same way, pick an age and think about it.

Sit and imagine that you are traveling to another city or to someone's home. What do you see? Explore the site in detail. Look for unusual objects or things taking place. Check out what you saw with the actual location.

Imagine that someone whom you know is a rose. How does the rose look? Is it a new bud, barely open, or is it fully developed? Look at the stem and where the base of the rose is. Is it in water, a vase, the earth, or just in the air? What does this tell you about the person? Ask your mind for the answer. The first thing that comes to you is usually the correct answer.

We don't give our heart and mind credit for knowing an answer or for being able to interpret the information it has given us. For example, you might ask a question about someone using the rose exercise above. Let us imagine that instead of seeing a red rose you saw a white rose that was fully open. Perhaps your first inclination is to say, "I don't know what that means." Ask. You will immediately hear something like white means age, enlightenment, health, etc., and that fully open implies an open individual. Trust the information that you receive.

You must begin to trust yourself.

If you do not then you will forever be looking to others to prove your own merit to you, and you will never be satisfied.

You will always be asking others what to do, and at the same time resenting those from whom you seek such aid.

—Jane Roberts,
The Nature of Personal Reality

CHAPTER NINE

Trust

We have been conditioned by our society that what we can't see, touch, taste, or feel doesn't exist. Our educational system values analytical reasoning. Little support is given the artistic or creative child unless they attend a special school for the gifted and talented.

Our religious institutions have instilled the concept of a God who sits in heaven with a long, grey beard and doles out rewards and punishments according to our acts in life. In western society, no value is given to the possibility that just maybe this isn't the only life we have led, that just maybe we aren't expected to get it perfect in one single time around.

It is little wonder that after all of this conditioning we find ourselves unable to trust that thought that pops into our head, or that feeling that seems to come out of the blue but brings with it good, valuable information.

Trusting your intuition automatically implies that you must take a risk. You must risk being wrong, or having your friends think you are foolish because you can't give a rational reason for what you are doing, and possibly losing friends because they can't stand to be with someone who does things, in their eyes, on a whim. You must risk change in yourself, in relationships, in your environment. You must risk that you will find more to life than you ever thought existed, that you do have answers—answers that work and are meaningful. You must risk your security in order to know that the inner voice guides and directs you in every facet of your life and while you may not always be able to see where you are going, you trust your intuition and know that you are in the right place at the right time.

Begin to get in touch with your inner voice by learning how you receive your answers. Remember that there are many different ways that intuitive information is received. Do you have a thought suddenly pop into your head? Are you able to check the thought out to see if the information is valid? Feedback is very important in learning to trust ourselves. If your intuition says take a warm coat even though the thermometer is reading 80 degrees, do you take the coat or do you rationalize just why you couldn't possibly need a coat in weather like this? Either way, when a freak snowstorm hits, you have verification that your inner voice was accurate.

Intuition speaks softly and is very patient. You may hear, and ignore, the same message again and again. It doesn't make demands or try to make you feel guilty. You may be hearing the message while you are driving home from work or out running. It doesn't necessarily come when you sit down and meditate, you may not be relaxed in this state, or you may be trying too hard to receive your answer.

Learn to act on your physical feelings, the barometer discussed earlier. When you start to listen to your physical body and follow what it tells you, you begin to get in the flow of knowing the answers and the questions.

Ask for help from the Universe. Many individuals feel that they can only ask for help in matters of a highly spiritual nature. You are in this physical body for a reason. Your inner voice is a part of your physical body and is as interested in whether or not you are following a diet that is healthy to you as in whether you can meditate for forty minutes and see your guardians and the white light.

Look for external signs of verification as well as internal. Sometimes, if we have been ignoring our inner wisdom, we may find a friend saying something to us that we have been hearing, but ignoring, for months. Or someone may give you a book that just happens to have the answer you have been looking for. There are many ways to receive information if we are open to them.

Learn to pay attention to your "awareness." What are you aware of at this moment? Focus your awareness on your body. What is tense? What is relaxed? How are you holding your shoulders? Your head? Your upper arms?

Is this awareness something inside or a fantasy? Direct your awareness to something you are not presently aware of. Is it inside or outside of yourself?

Next, direct your attention to the small toe on your left foot. What are you aware of now? Are you aware of the small toe on your right foot?

Let your awareness wander. See where it takes you.

There are many ways that we sabotage our intuition. For example:

Intuition: I would like to separate from my business partner and go out on my own.

Something doesn't feel right here.

Rational: I'll never succeed on my own. I'll be financially strapped, I'll lose his friendship.

Intuition: Although I know the party tonight will be talked about for weeks, I would rather stay home and read.

Rational: People will think I'm not being social. The hostess will think I don't like him/ her. I should go, it's the proper thing to do.

Intuition: Call Robert.

Rational: Robert will think I'm chasing him, trying to trap him, pestering him. (It may actually be fact that Robert wants to talk to you but hasn't been able to reach you.)

You get the idea. One can always think of rational reasons why they shouldn't do what their intuition tells them to do. Often the most commonly used rational excuse is that "it isn't logical." Logic does not always go hand in hand with your intuitive voice.

QUESTIONS

Q: There are times when I follow my intuition and it turns out to be wrong. How can I tell when it is right and when it is wrong?

A: Your intuition is always right, but there are times when we misinterpret what we see or sense. We may think that we "see" a beautiful swimming pool when, in fact, we see a sewage treatment facility. As you learn how your mind brings information to you, you will be able to use your mental pictures or sounds along with your physical feelings. The combination will help you interpret your information accurately. Always know that you can ask your dreams to bring you the answer, because it is not as easy to control and manipulate our dreams.

Q: It is easy for me to trust what a psychic tells me, but when it comes to my own inner wisdom I fall short. How can I change this?

A: When you consistently give your power away to someone who you think has all of the answers, especially for yourself, you are giving your intuition the message that you don't trust it. Begin to "listen" to your intuition on a daily basis and follow the advice it gives. With each act of faith your own intuitive process will become stronger. Only when you feel you need someone to reflect back to you what you are creating, or when you feel that your emotions are clouding your answers, should you seek answers from a source outside of yourself. Even then, see how the answers that you are given resonate with your inner being.

Q: When I get answers from inside, I think that I am just making it up. How do I know when I'm not, that it's not just my imagination?

A: You are making it up, but your imagination is real.

You can call it guessing if you like . . . but you want to learn to "guess" with a ninety-five percent accuracy rate. Don't worry about whether or not you are making it up, we make everything up, including our entire lives!

MEDITATION

Sit quietly in a place where you feel very comfortable. Close your eyes and watch or listen to the thoughts that travel through your mind. Pay attention, but do not hold on to any one particular thought, just let it pass by as a cloud would drift across the sky. Notice your inner feelings about these thoughts. Do you feel anxious, comfortable, or neutral? Move your awareness to your heart and see how it feels right now. Imagine that your heart is radiating white light out from you and into the Universe. Repeat the following affirmation to your heart and to the Universe:

"I know that there is more to life than what can be seen. I want to get in touch with this knowledge and to learn to trust it. I am willing to travel where I cannot see and know what I cannot know. I am willing to listen to the voice that has no sound and to the message of my heart. I trust."

Continue to sit quietly and ask yourself these questions:

- What is keeping me from trusting my intuition at this point in my life?
- What previously kept me from trusting my intuition?
- What do I need to do right now to increase my trust in myself?
- To whom do I give away my "power?" (Whom do you trust with answers more than you trust yourself?)
- When was the last time I heard an intuitive message and acted on it?

When was the last time I heard an intuitive message and didn't act on it?

Tell yourself that you will remember these answers and use them to help you further your own intuitive awareness and trust of yourself. Thank your "heart" for its help in this meditation.

EXERCISE

The next time you feel you have an intuitive hunch about something . . . *act* on it. See what happens. If it was from your heart it will prove to be good, valuable information. If it was off the mark, e.g., your ego talking, the information may prove less than accurate or complete. Remember how you felt when you got the information, did you take it to your heart and see how it felt there?

"The moment one definitely commits oneself, then Providence moves too. All sorts of things occur to help one that would never otherwise have occurred. A whole stream of events issues from the decision which no man could have dreamed would have come his way. Whatever you can do, or dream you can do, begin it. Boldness has genius, power, and magic in it. Begin it now."

—Goethe

CHAPTER TEN

Intention

Someone takes a step, commits oneself, and things begin to happen. Is it because we are able to "read" our future and we set goals? Do we work hard, make money and purchase our desires? Or does our world manifest because we create it? Does it make any difference?

Many books and articles have been written about the power of the mind and of visualization. The popular book, *The Secret,* took an ancient message that we don't understand, forced it through our material culture, and made a lot of money for the authors/producers. Do its tenants work for everyone? Perhaps it works temporarily for some people.

If we truly believed that we are responsible for what happens to us on Earth, and for what we do on Earth after we leave it, we would do things differently. By not trusting in our greatness we create pain, suffering, and war because we have not learned to create anything else.

When we create unconsciously, we recreate the past: the same painful relationships, the same sense of being victim, the same sense of being unworthy, until we wake up and say, "I have been creating this, I'm not going to do this anymore."

This chapter is titled "Intention" because intention is a willful and conscious action. Intention is not just a thought, a thing, an action, or an ambition, but an alignment with Spirit. Everyone has stories to tell about how something they wanted showed up, whether it is through "imaging" the outcome, making a storyboard, or praying.

There are many *manifesting* stories that I could share, but most of these stories ultimately left me with more questions than answers. My most significant *intending* happened several years ago when I was attempting to play golf with Michael. For the record, I am not a golfer and I spent most of that day tilling the greens. Toward the end of the game, I thought about my father, who was a golfer. He used to tell me, "Golf is like the game of life. Every round is a journey, which ultimately leads you back to where you began, hopefully a little wiser. The ball is a symbol of perfection. It contains all potential because it is a sphere. When it is in flight it is a reminder to us that we can fly if we put our minds to it. If you can learn to focus your mind and send that little ball exactly where you want it to go, then you can focus your life and create it exactly as you would have it. In this simple game is hidden the true secret of life."

Closing my eyes and setting my intention, I immediately visualized a very sharp, focused, and detailed moving picture of the golf ball rolling 25 feet over the green, toward the hole and dropping in.

It's hard to describe, but I was totally absorbed in that moment. There was a clarity that I can't explain. My perspective was at the ground level, looking at the golf ball in front of me. There were only four things in the entire Universe—pure awareness, the golf ball, the putter, and the hole. I opened my eyes, gripped the putter, and putted.

As if pulled by an unseen filament of destiny, the golf ball rolled exactly as I had imagined. It rolled 25 feet to the hole and dropped in.

In the grand scheme of things, whether or not I sank the golf ball is of little importance. But on my path of understanding, it was critical. I learned, through direct experience, how intent and imagery create our reality. No other thought came into my mind between my image of the path of the golf ball and my putt. For a brief moment in time, I stretched beyond my boundaries —touched the inconceivable . . . and an extraordinary even took place.

How did this happen? It would seem that all of the elements of manifesting, of *real* magic, were there. I had a well-defined intent, yet I was not attached to the outcome. I wasn't playing for the Master's cup. I was simply attempting something that my father once suggested: "Focus your mind and send your golf ball exactly where you want it to go."

In that moment there were no conflicting desires that would cancel out my intent, which was simple—the golf ball drops into the hole. Because my awareness was expanded, my intellect could not jump in and separate me from my intent, giving me all the distractions available.

Still, there was something else that took place on that green, in that moment when my state of mind was graced by extraordinary clarity. For the briefest of instants, I stepped into a magic realm that, I believe, has been here all along.*

(Excerpt from *A Hidden Order*)

EXERCISE

First, let me be perfectly clear that even though I have had numerous times when what I intended happened, I have no idea how it works. Yes, many things in my life were originally just a dim thought, and they came to pass. But if all of our thoughts materialized we would have a lot of dead lawyers, husbands, wives, and enemies. What follows are guidelines for you to play with. Perhaps you will find more pieces to the puzzle and even surprise yourself with the results.

Have clear intent. Know what you want. Know that you have to devote some time to the thought in order to get what you want. Then release it. (Non-attachment is very important. You must release what it is that you want. It has to reach the energy of the Universe in order for it to come back to you.)

Byron Gentry, a healer from Oklahoma, used clapping to help manifest health, etc. (I use a combination of things I learned from Byron, from Shakti Gawain, and from my own source of wisdom.) Have a clear picture of what it is you want to manifest. Clap once to put your head in a positive polarity and your feet in a negative polarity. Clap three times to dissolve any emotional energy around the situation, and then clap five times to increase the *velocity* of Universal energy coming into your body. Finally, clap five times to increase the *amount* of Universal energy coming into your body.

Picture or feel the situation, as you would like it to be. Neville

Goddard said it was not what we want to attract, but rather that we attract what we believe to be true. He was also convinced that Scripture was rife with this idea that man had to *think from the end.* He called it the state of **I AM**, this being a mystical translation of the name of God. Man could attain any goal, he reasoned, provided he adopted the feeling of it in the present. (*The* Neville Reader.)

Be sure to put yourself in the picture. Put this picture in a pink balloon, take it to your favorite spot and release it and as you say: "This, or something better, now manifests for me in perfectly satisfying and harmonious ways for the highest good of all concerned."

After a while there may be instances when you will wonder if you are actually creating your life, or fantastically in tune with what the Universe is sending your way. When you are in harmony with the Universe you will realize it doesn't make any difference. Things will work out exactly as they are supposed to, and on schedule.

The simplest way to manifest is to ask—ask the Universe, your highest source of information, to help you. Ask her to help you get information from your dreams, to experience or to be aware of an out-of-body state, to know what it is you are supposed to be doing. Remember, as you are asking, you have to continue to put forth some energy on your own behalf in order to move towards your goal.

CHAPTER ELEVEN

The Game

In the end it all boils down to the fact that life is just a game, a magnificent game that we are playing. As we play the game we invent the rules, and one of the rules is the fact that it is never too late to change the road we are traveling. Intuition helps us know or create the rules and change the rules or the road.

One: You chose to be here, so be here now.

Living in the moment is everything. All too often we're living in the past, or the future, but not the now. Do you know what it's like to take a walk and enjoy where you are at that point in time, without letting your mind race ahead to what you have to do when you return? It's difficult for us, as human beings, to keep our thoughts only on the present. We have been programmed to look backward or forward in time. Only when we are in the present can we create the future, sounds paradoxical, but it's true.

Being here now means enjoying exactly where you are at any given time. Don't be anxious for tomorrow, it will be here soon enough. Then you will be looking ahead to next week or next month or next year. Tomorrow will take care of itself, but today you can be here and feel the heart-felt messages that come to you in the now. Look at it this way . . . what if there is no tomorrow? What if the only thing you can be sure of is today? What then? Would you do things differently? Would you be angry at someone you love? Would you be so obsessive about whether or not the breakfast dishes were washed or the lawn mowed? Would you refrain from telling someone that you love him or her?

Two: Because you chose to be here, you also chose your body, your parents, your friends and your present life situation. No one has done anything to you, but you. There may be times when you are unable to see what you were supposed to get out of a given situation, but you can rest assured that when you are in your total state of knowing you set up the situation and lessons you wanted to learn this time around.

Three: You get what you need. The law of the Universe—our own ability to create and manifest— gives us what we need, not necessarily what we want.

Four: Whatever you think of strongly, or put your energies into, you attract into your life. If you are negative in your attitude, then you will attract people and circumstances in your life to reinforce that belief system. If, on the other hand, you are a positive, optimistic person, your life will reflect back to you one of divine order, happiness, and well-being.

Five: The Universe is abundant, but we live in a material, finite world, which (at some level) we have created. Being human, we have a responsibility to take care of the earth and all of her creatures.

Six: You will have magnificent bursts of spiritual growth, to be followed by what seems to be a period of quiet. It is during these times of quiet that the most is happening; this is when your unconscious is being its most creative. Part of our learning in this lifetime is to learn patience. This means not forcing the rose, but letting it unfold in its own time.

Seven: "You cannot discover new oceans until you have the courage to lose sight of the shore." (Author unknown)

Eight: Realize that you are asleep, trying to wake up. In so doing you will begin to unravel the mysteries of life and open your heart.

Nine: The only thing you know is what you don't know. In fact, you don't know what you don't know!

Ten: *To everything there is a season, and a time to every purpose under the heaven.*

—Ecclesiastes 3:1

Eleven: *Ask, and it shall be given you, seek, and ye shall find, knock, and it shall be opened unto you.*

—Matthew 7:7

TIPS FOR MOVING BEYOND INTUITION

- *Let go of self-importance. You do not have to compete or push ahead of others to obtain your desires. Excessive force in one direction triggers the growth of an opposing force. Several times a day stop and be still. Listen.*
- *Create your own ideology. Do not rely on what you have read, or have been taught. Discover for yourself.*
- *Play with the idea that you are creating everything in your life. Don't wait for someone, or something else, to tell you what direction to head in. (This includes taking responsibility for the person you just had an argument with, the fact you got fired, or climate disruption.)*
- *Notice where you are, what you have, and if your current reality is consistent with what you want in the future.*
- *Whatever you want to do with your life, decide . . . start now, and do it one step at a time.*
- *Allow Life to happen. Life is change, do not fear it. Stay open and attentive and do not try to hold on to that which wishes to change.*
- *Move on. Nothing is stagnant in nature.*

SUGGESTED READING

In this 2015 edition of *Intuitions*, there are many wonderful books about intuition, and consciousness. I encourage you to follow what calls you. The following are some of my all-time favorites with timeless information.

Castaneda, Carlos. *The Power of Silence*. New York, N.Y: Simon & Schuster, 1987.

Dominguez, Joe & Vicki Robin. *Your Money or Your Life*. New York, N.Y: Viking Penguin, 1992.

Goldstein, Joseph. *Insight Meditation*. Boston and London: Shambala, 1993.

Kabat-Zinn, John. *Wherever You Go, There You Are*. New York: Hyperion, 1994.

Robinson, Winter. *A Hidden Order*. Boston, MA: Redwheel/Weiser, 2004.

Russell, Peter. *The White Hole in Time*. San Francisco, CA: Harper, 1992.

Talbot, Michael. *The Holographic Universe*. New York, NY: Harper Collins, 1991.

McCammon, Robert R. *Boy's Life*. New York, NY: Pocket Books, 1991.

Murphy, Michael. *The Future of the Body*. Los Angeles, CA: Jeremy P. Tarcher, Inc., 1992.

ORGANIZATIONS CLOSE TO MY HEART

Dolphin Research Center
P.O. Box 2875 Marathon Shores, FL 33052
dolphins.org

The Monroe Institute
365 Roberts Mountain Road
Faber, Virginia 22958
Monroeinstitute.org

Wild Dolphin Project
21 Hepburn Avenue, Suite 20
Jupiter, FL 33458
wilddolphinproject.org

ABOUT THE AUTHOR

WINTER ROBINSON, M.Ed., is internationally recognized as an author, teacher, consultant and medical intuitive, adept at facilitating the intuitive process, multi-sensory development and exploring human consciousness. A licensed therapist, she is the author of *A Hidden Order: Uncover Your Life's Design*; *Intuitions: Seeing with the Heart*; and *Remembering: A Gentle Reminder of Who You Are*. She has also created a series of guided imagery CDs to help the listener reduce stress and deepen the alliance with the source of inner wisdom. A board-certified therapist who graduated from the University of Virginia (M.Ed.), Winter began her career as a therapist at the Addiction Research Foundation (Toronto). She headed up a pilot study facilitating the art of medicine (medical intuition) to medical students at Brown University. For many years Winter was a TMI residential trainer and a research subject in the institute lab.

You can find her online at www.winterrobinson.com

Curious about other Crossroad Press books?
Stop by our site:
http://store.crossroadpress.com
We offer quality writing
in digital, audio, and print formats.

Enter the code FIRSTBOOK
to get 20% off your first order from our store!
Stop by today!

Printed in Great Britain
by Amazon

83657288R00068